OVERVIEW

Overview

It was a terrifying scene: A lone gunman was holding several adults and children hostage on a New York subway. It seemed certain someone would be wounded or shot, when a male passenger, no bigger in size than the gunman himself, tackled the criminal and seized his weapon. This heroic act gives us insight into the purpose and intensity of human emotions.

This type of gesture suggests that deep feelings and emotions act as necessary guides when humans face situations too important to defer to the intellect alone. Situations that arouse such emotional responses include:
- facing danger,
- suffering a painful loss,
- pursuing goals despite frustration,
- bonding with fellow humans,
- building a family.

Question
Is the following statement true or false?

In situations that require decision-making, emotions do not count as much as logic does.
Options:
1. true
2. false

Answer:
Actually, emotions and logic both count in decision-making.

Option 1: This statement is not true. In situations involving decision-making, relying on logic alone is not as smart as relying on emotions and rational thought together.

Option 2: This statement is false. In all decision-making and action situations, feelings count as much, if not more, than rational thought.

In all decision-making and action situations, feelings count as much, if not more, than rational thought. In fact, there has been far too much emphasis on rational thought (IQ) in the past when evaluating human behavior and potential.

In this book you'll gain an understanding of the emotional intelligence theory, and you'll explore the basis of emotional intelligence by examining the following four areas:
- the purpose of emotions,
- managing emotions,
- the impact of emotional intelligence,
- what it takes to become emotionally literate.

Can you measure your intelligence simply by taking an IQ test? Will your SAT scores determine your on-the-job success?

Question

Actually, most studies show that IQ doesn't accurately predict workplace success. There are other factors that influence success on the job. Which of the given factors do you think influence work effectiveness?

Options:
1. a good understanding of yourself and your abilities
2. the ability to motivate yourself
3. the skills to manage your emotions
4. the ability to "read" people and their emotions

Answer:
Actually, your understanding of yourself and others is an important factor. Your skills in motivating yourself, managing your emotions, and understanding the emotions of others help you stand out from your peers.

Option 1: This answer is correct. Having a good understanding of yourself and your abilities will help you stand out on the job because knowing your strengths and weaknesses means you are honest with yourself and others around you.

Option 2: This answer is correct. Being self-motivated influences your success on the job because you believe in what the company stands for and you strive to meet and exceed company goals.

Option 3: This answer is correct. Being able to manage your emotions influences your success on the job because you will be proactive in difficult situations and will interact productively and appropriately with clients and co-workers.

Option 4: This answer is correct. Understanding the emotions of others will influence your success on the job because you will be able to anticipate others' needs and moods.

Studies show that emotional intelligence plays a role that's just as, if not more, important than IQ. By developing your people skills, you'll have a positive effect on your career. In this book, you'll explore:
- what emotional intelligence is,
- how to realistically evaluate yourself,
- why it's important to manage your emotions,
- how self-motivation affects your career.

Groups are common in the workplace. Why do some work groups flourish, while others seem to drag behind?

Team members develop a culture which contributes strongly to their success. Some groups have an atmosphere of excitement and an ability to adapt. Others resist change and have a negative, growth-inhibiting environment.

The ability to handle emotions appropriately and work well with others is known as emotional intelligence. This competency factors into the team's success.

Participation and collaboration are key to the success of your team. In this book, you'll explore the importance of these characteristics in accomplishing group goals. You'll also examine:

- the competencies needed to become an effective team member,
- the techniques for handling emotions,
- the ways to evaluate your team's emotional intelligence,
- the strategies for improving your team's emotional intelligence.

Stellar teams don't appear out of thin air. They're made up of the right people in the right place. These teams have the support and encouragement they need to succeed. Team members are committed to the success of the group and they work to enhance their abilities to thrive in today's fast-paced business environment. This book will help you contribute effectively to your team's growth.

Are the most successful people "intellectuals"? Or do they have a different kind of brainpower that helps them excel in the workplace?

How can you increase your "people smarts"? First, you'll need a strong understanding of emotional intelligence. Then, you will need to understand how and what you need to improve. In this book, you'll examine:
- how emotional and intellectual intelligence differ,
- why emotional intelligence matters at work,
- where emotional intelligence comes from,
- how to improve your emotional intelligence.

In today's workplace, you need emotional intelligence to get along with others. The "stars" around you outshine others because of their ability to use their emotions effectively. Most people believe that emotions are automatic responses over which they have no control. Actually, emotions are determined by what you think. There are concrete techniques to help you gain control of your feelings. In this book, you'll gain the skills needed to increase your emotional intelligence.

Emotional intelligence is a popular concept. How does it relate to your effectiveness as a leader? This book delves into the importance of emotional intelligence to today's leaders. You'll examine:
- why leaders need emotional intelligence,
- how you can acquire emotional intelligence,
- why it's important to develop your staff,

- how you can increase others' emotional intelligence.

This book will provide you with a step-by-step guide to increasing your effectiveness as a leader. You'll learn proven techniques for improving your relationship with your staff. You will also examine leadership strategies for getting more work done with less stress.

CHAPTER I - DEFINING EMOTIONAL INTELLIGENCE

CHAPTER I - Defining Emotional Intelligence

In this chapter you'll gain an understanding of the emotional intelligence theory, and you'll explore the basis of emotional intelligence by examining the following four areas:

- the purpose of emotions,
- managing emotions,
- the impact of emotional intelligence,
- what it takes to become emotionally literate.

THE PURPOSE OF EMOTIONS

The Purpose of Emotions
What's happening inside the brain when someone is moved to tears? What reactions and actions are taking place internally when an individual becomes enraged? How is it that someone with an average IQ can be wildly successful, while an individual with a high IQ flounders miserably?

Questions like these, which focus more on the emotional aspects of life, have fascinated the scientific community for years.

Dramatic new research has provided neurobiological data that provide glimpses of the inner workings of the brain. These data are clarifying how the emotional control center works, disputing the long-held belief that IQ determines success.

Qualities like self-control, motivation, and persistence--emotional intelligence--are now being proved to be equally as, if not more, important than IQ.

Question

Why are these "emotional intelligence" qualities so important in determining an individual's intelligence? Select all those that identify the importance of emotional intelligence.

Options:

1. Emotional intelligence contributes to an individual's ability to self-motivate.

2. IQ scores can be increased by increasing emotional intelligence.

3. Emotional intelligence plays a significant role in impulse control.

4. Emotions override logic in highly emotional moments.

Answer:

Actually, emotional intelligence is associated with all of the mentioned areas, except increasing IQ scores.

Option 1: Correct. An important aspect of emotional intelligence is that it contributes to an individual's ability to self-motivate. For example, someone with a high IQ can be less successful than someone who is highly motivated and has a lower IQ.

Option 2: This answer is incorrect. Emotional intelligence has no impact on IQ scores.

Option 3: This answer is correct. Impulse control (or self-control) is just one of several characteristics that predict and measure emotional intelligence--which is equally as important as IQ, if not more so.

Option 4: This answer is correct. In highly emotional moments, the body is conditioned to respond with emotion rather than logic. Consider, for example, the "flight or fight" response.

In this lesson, "The Purpose of Emotions," you'll gain an understanding of the important role that emotions play in determining the success of an individual's life experience. You'll explore the following areas:
- how emotions function,
- how the emotional control center works,
- how emotional intelligence compares to IQ.

Maria awoke with a start. Her blood ran cold and all her senses were on alert. She quickly scanned the house, searching for the source of her concern. Just seconds earlier, she had been awakened by the sound of shattering glass. Was someone in the house? Had an intruder crept in? As her cat Muffy meowed, Maria saw her favorite vase shattered on the dining room floor. She breathed a sigh of relief as she realized that Muffy, not an intruder, had caused the noise.

Maria's physical response was a result of her fear. Physical reactions like this are embedded in the nervous system. For primitive humans, these reactions were often the difference between life and death. Today, they can clash with rational responses. In this segment, you'll learn the physiological responses to:
- anger
- fear
- love and happiness
- surprise
- disgust and sadness

Each emotion is an impulse to act. You may have heard this referred to as the "fight or flight" reaction. Every emotion has a unique role in preparing the body for some type of response. One of the strongest emotions people feel is anger.

See each physiological response to anger for more information.

The "fight" response

When a person is angry, blood flows to the hands. The original purpose was to facilitate grasping a weapon--the "fight" response.

Adrenaline

When angry, the heart rate increases, and there is a rush of adrenaline that creates a surge of energy for intense action.

Closely aligned with anger is fear--the "flight" response. A rush of hormones puts the body on general alert, causing it to freeze temporarily and then making it ready for action. Blood flows away from the face and to the large muscles, making it easier to run. Responses like these allowed primitive humans to concentrate on the threat at hand and decide whether to hide or flee. These physiological responses still occur, even though modern culture doesn't normally require such actions.

To identify your "fight or flight" response, consider how you might react if someone unexpectedly started banging on your car window while you were waiting at a stoplight. You'd probably freeze momentarily, grip the wheel a little tighter, and quickly begin evaluating your options.

Question

Which emotions are involved in the "fight or flight" response?

Options:

1. anger
2. fear
3. surprise
4. disgust

Answer:

The correct responses show the two emotions that trigger the "fight or flight" mobilization.

Option 1: This answer is correct. Anger triggers the "fight or flight" response because when a person is angry, blood flows to the hands and the heart rate increases, both of which prepare an individual during a fight to attack or defend themselves.

Option 2: Correct. Fear is involved in the "fight or flight" response. Blood flows away from the face and to the large muscles, making it easier to run, which allowed primitive humans to concentrate on the threat at hand and decide whether to hide or flee.

Option 3: This is incorrect. Surprise is not involved in the "fight or flight" response, although it is one among a spectrum of emotions that triggers a strong physiological response.

Option 4: This is incorrect. Disgust is not involved in the "fight or flight" response. Curling the upper lip and wrinkling the nose is primitive humans' attempt to resist a noxious odor or spit out a poisonous food.

Anger and fear are part of a spectrum of emotions. Other emotions that trigger different physiological responses are love and happiness, surprise, disgust, and sadness. Keep in mind that although people don't always display their emotions, the underlying physiological reaction is present.

See each of the other core emotions that are ingrained in humans for more information.

Love and happiness

Love and happiness are exhibited by a general sense of calmness and contentment. Brain signals inhibit negative feelings and foster an increase in energy.

Disgust

Disgust is revealed by curling the upper lip and wrinkling the nose--primitive humans' attempt to resist a noxious odor or spit out a poisonous food.

Sadness

Sadness produces a decrease in energy and enthusiasm and slows the body's metabolism. It is often accompanied by a flow of tears.

Surprise

The body responds to surprise by lifting the eyebrows to permit more light to reach the retina and allow a wider range of view. This met primitive humans' needs to assess the unexpected event and create a plan for action.

Question

Emotions can cause a variety of physiological responses, some of which are listed here. Match each emotion with one or more responses that it creates.

Options:

A. disgust
B. sadness
C. fear
D. love

Targets:

1. nose wrinkles slightly
2. body put on general alert
3. cooperation facilitated
4. tears flow
5. body freezes

Answer:

A physiological response to disgust is the nose wrinkling slightly, which is the primitive humans' attempt to resist a noxious odor.

A physiological response to fear is the body put on general alert, making it ready for action. Blood flows away from the face and to the large muscles, making it easier to run.

A physiological response to love is cooperation is facilitated and a general sense of calmness and contentment is present. Brain signals inhibit negative feelings and foster an increase in energy.

A physiological response to sadness is tears flowing. There is a decrease in energy and enthusiasm and slowing of the body's metabolism, which is often accompanied by a flow of tears.

A physiological response to fear is the body freezes, which allowed primitive humans to concentrate on the threat at hand and decide whether to hide or flee.

Physical reactions have been implanted in the nervous system since primitive times. While they originally served as a survival mechanism, in modern society the emotions listed here can obscure rational thinking and cloud judgment.

- anger
- fear
- love and happiness
- surprise
- disgust
- sadness

Bob and Deidrea were discussing a recent event in Deidrea's career. Deidrea had been passed over for a promotion that she felt sure she would get. Three months later, she had adjusted to the idea and was enjoying her current position.

However, when she said to Bob, "I'm glad I didn't get promoted. Who wants that kind of stress in life?" her voice cracked and her eyes welled up slightly.

The incident just described could easily go unnoticed, but to the emotionally aware individual, the message was twofold: Deidrea's rational mind was thoughtfully reflecting upon her experience. However, Deidrea's emotional mind, which is more impulsive and sometimes illogical, was more powerful and contradicted her words.

Both the rational and the emotional mind were at work when Deidrea was talking to Bob.

All humans have two minds, so to speak: the emotional mind and the rational mind. These two minds are often called the head and the heart. To more fully explore the functions of the emotional control center, you will learn:

- how the emotional mind functions,
- how the rational mind functions,
- how the emotional and rational minds interact.

Your emotional mind and your rational mind interact to construct your mental life. Usually, the emotional mind and the rational mind operate in harmony and balance.

See each type of mind for more information on its function.

Emotional mind

The emotional mind is located in the amygdala and feeds into the rational mind, guiding its operations.

Rational mind

The rational mind, located in the neocortex, refines and sometimes overrules the input of the emotional mind.

While the amygdala and neocortex usually work in tandem, the amygdala overtakes the rational mind when emotions are running high. In highly emotional moments, the amygdala plays a crucial role in how a person reacts.

Select each amygdala function to reveal what happened when Dale encountered some shady looking characters while walking to his car late one evening.

scanning

Dale's amygdala began processing sensory signals to determine if the situation was threatening. If it was, his amygdala would send warning messages to other parts of the brain and body.

alerting

If Dale deemed the situation were threatening, his amygdala would serve as a watchdog to quickly alert his body to prepare for action.

facilitating response

While serving as the watchdog, Dale's amygdala would facilitate his body's fight or flight response by releasing the necessary hormones that allow for quick movement and thinking.

overtaking rationale

In addition to scanning, alerting, and facilitating responses, Dale's amygdala would overtake and control most of the brain, including his neocortex (or rational mind).

A fascinating example of the amygdala's ability to motivate movement was seen in a news story. A woman in an electric wheelchair was crossing the railroad tracks when her chair became stuck in the tracks with a train quickly approaching. A passing driver saw her predicament, jumped out of his car, and freed the chair

Emotional Intelligence at Work

just seconds before the train roared by. Although the chair was damaged, neither the woman nor the good samaritan was injured. What made this man jeopardize his own life to save a stranger? The amygdala.

Question

The brain's emotional control center is a crucial factor in emotional intelligence. Which statements describe how the emotional control center works?

Options:

1. The emotional control center is located in the amygdala.
2. The neocortex is responsible for all emotional memories.
3. The hippocampus constantly monitors events for possible trouble.
4. The amygdala sounds an alarm to various parts of the body when a problem is detected.

Answer:

The emotional control center is located in the amygdala, which is responsible for emotional memories. The amygdala acts like a sentinel, watching over events.

Option 1: This answer is correct. The emotional mind or control center is located in the amygdala and feeds into the rational mind, guiding its operations.

Option 2: This answer is incorrect. The neocortex is involved in rational, not emotional thought. It refines and sometimes overrules the input of the emotional mind.

Option 3: This answer is incorrect. The hippocampus is involved in neither emotional nor rational thought.

Option 4: This choice is correct. The emotional control center sounds an alarm to various parts of the body when a problem is detected, which quickly alerts the body to prepare for action.

Your two minds--the head and the heart--are always present in every situation you encounter. How each situation is experienced is dependent upon the degree of emotion involved and the areas just explored:
- how the emotional mind works,
- how the rational mind works,
- how the emotional and rational minds interact.

Dave and John are recent college graduates. Dave's IQ is 20 points higher than John's; he is impatient and wants everything immediately. On the other hand, John can curb his short-term desires if it means reaching a bigger goal. Furthermore, John has had an ability to empathize with others since childhood.

Who do you think scored higher on his SAT exam for college entrance? Who do you think will be more successful in his career?

John scored higher on his SAT and likely will be more successful in his career. He possesses a higher degree of emotional intelligence, which is a better predictor of life success than IQ. In this segment, you'll learn:
- the elements of emotional intelligence and IQ,
- the traits of people with high emotional intelligence or IQ,
- how each person's intelligence contributes to life success.

IQ measures a person's intellectual ability and generally remains steady throughout life. It contributes to about 20 percent of the factors that determine life success. Traits exhibited by a person with a high IQ include a wide intellectual capacity and range of interests, confidence and fluency in expressing thoughts and opinions, a tendency to be anxious and to worry, and a critical nature. IQ is comprised of several mental abilities.

Review each mental ability for its definition.

verbal comprehension - the ability to understand and define words

word fluency - the ability to think of words rapidly, such as quickly completing a crossword puzzle or making an extemporaneous speech

number facility - the ability to do mathematical problems

spatial ability - the ability to visualize objects and draw them from memory

memory - the ability to memorize and recall information

perception - the ability to notice details and detect similarities and differences

reasoning - the ability to follow general rules

Emotional intelligence is comprised of a broad range of abilities including awareness of one's own emotions, the ability to regulate moods, the recognition of emotions in others, the ability to motivate oneself in the face of frustration, the ability to control impulses and delay gratification, and the ability to empathize. Emotional intelligence contributes to about 80 percent of the factors that predict life success.

Jeffery, who possesses high emotional intelligence, is poised, outgoing, and cheerful. He has empathy for others, expresses his feelings directly but appropriately, and has a capacity for developing relationships.

Case Study: Question 1 of 3

Scenario

For your convenience, the case study is repeated with each question.

This case study depicts emotional intelligence and IQ in action. Mark and Christie work together. Christie is confident and opinionated--and she's usually right. She has brilliant ideas but often rubs people the wrong way. To most observers, Mark appears reserved and uninvolved. However, he often has insightful comments at meetings and is particularly skilled at getting teams to function effectively. Christie and Mark have encountered a problem. Christie struggles to solve it by herself, while Mark picks up the phone and calls a trusted colleague.

Consider Mark's and Christie's level of emotional intelligence by answering the questions.

Question

Which one of the two people in the case study appears to have a higher level of emotional intelligence?

Options:

1. Mark
2. Christie

Answer:

Actually, Mark is the individual who is displaying a higher level of emotional intelligence.

Option 1: Correct. Mark has the higher level of emotional intelligence because he exhibits the ability to regulate moods, the ability to motivate himself and others, and the ability to empathize. When confronted with a problem, he does not panic.

Option 2: Incorrect. Christie has a lower level of emotional intelligence because she is confident and opinionated--and she's usually right. She has brilliant ideas but often rubs people the wrong way and struggles with the problem she has encountered.

Case Study: Question 2 of 3

Which of the traits demonstrate Mark's emotional intelligence?

Options:

1. excels at team building
2. is prone to anxiety
3. draws attention to himself
4. observes and draws conclusions

Answer:

Team building and the ability to observe and draw conclusions demonstrate Mark's emotional intelligence.

Option 1: This answer is correct. One of the traits that demonstrates Mark's emotional intelligence is that he excels at team building. This is possible because he has a capacity for developing relationships and the ability to empathize.

Option 2: This answer is incorrect. Being prone to anxiety is not one of Mark's characteristics, and is more an example of high IQ than of emotional intelligence.

Option 3: This answer is incorrect because Mark, who has a high level of emotional intelligence, tends to appear reserved and uninvolved rather than drawing attention to himself.

Option 4: This answer is correct. Mark's emotional intelligence is evident because he observes and draws conclusions well, which means he is able to express his feelings directly but appropriately.

Case Study: Question 3 of 3

How might Christie be more successful at work by developing her emotional intelligence?

Options:
1. be more highly regarded for her ideas
2. solve problems more quickly
3. feel less anxious and critical

Answer

Christie could benefit by solving problems more quickly and feeling less anxious and critical.

Option 1: This answer is incorrect. Christie is already highly regarded for her ideas, but she often rubs people the wrong way, which is a characteristic of a high IQ and low emotional intelligence.

Option 2: Correct. By developing her emotional intelligence, Christie will be able to solve problems more quickly because she will be less critical and more willing to involve others in her decision making.

Option 3: This answer is correct. By developing her emotional intelligence, Christie will feel less anxious and critical because she will be better equipped to regulate moods.

Question

Differentiate between emotional intelligence and IQ. Match each type of intelligence with one or more appropriate statements.

Options:
A. emotional intelligence
B. IQ

Targets:
1. includes verbal comprehension and word fluency
2. is characterized by poise and cheerfulness
3. includes the ability to motivate yourself in the face of frustration

4. contributes 20 percent to the factors that determine success

5. is characterized by assertion and positive feelings about self

Answer:

IQ includes verbal comprehension (the ability to understand and define words), and word fluency (the ability to think of words rapidly).

Emotional intelligence is characterized by poise and cheerfulness, which is very important when relating to colleagues.

Emotional intelligence includes the ability to motivate yourself in the face of frustration. This characteristic is very important in a business setting when challenges are a regular occurrence.

IQ contributes 20 percent to the factors that determine success. It measures a person's intellectual ability and generally remains steady throughout life.

Emotional intelligence is characterized by assertion and positive feelings about self, which will help in getting ideas heard.

Emotional intelligence is a more accurate predictor of life success than IQ is. Fortunately, it's a skill that can be developed more readily than pure intellectual abilities. In this segment, you learned:

- the elements of emotional intelligence and IQ,
- the traits of people with high emotional intelligence or IQ,
- how each intelligence contributes to life success.
-

MANAGING EMOTIONS

Managing Emotions

Today, we call it "getting a grip." In earlier times, it was called temperance. Whatever the current term may be, the ability to cultivate appropriate emotional responses in a variety of settings is the essence of managing emotions.

Keeping your emotions balanced and being capable of restraining excess emotions is the key to your emotional well-being. Situations that provoke highly intensive emotions interfere with the ability to lead a productive, satisfying life. This doesn't mean you should strive to eliminate all emotional responses in your life; life by nature is a series of ups and downs, a mixture of joy and sadness, a combination of good and bad.

Developing the ability to garner appropriate emotional responses is a crucial life skill. Like it or not, you spend much of your life attempting to manage your moods and feelings.

Question

Achieving life balance requires having the ability to manage one's emotions. Which statements correctly identify the value of managing emotions?

Options:

1. Managing emotions enables you to avoid feeling bad.

2. Managing emotions will assist you in achieving emotional suppression.

3. Managing emotions will help you achieve balance.

4. Managing emotions enables you to limit the effects of anger and worry.

5. Managing emotions ensures life satisfaction and happiness.

6. Managing emotions is a critical skill in becoming emotionally intelligent.

Answer:

Actually, managing emotions enables you to limit the effects of anger and worry, achieve balance, and become more emotionally intelligent.

Option 1: This answer is incorrect. You may still feel bad depending on the situation, but managing emotions will keep these feelings appropriate.

Option 2: This answer is incorrect. If you suppress emotions, there will be no sense of balance.

Option 3: This answer is correct. Managing emotions will help you keep your emotions balanced. Being capable of restraining excess emotions is the key to emotional well-being.

Option 4: This answer is correct. Limiting the effects of anger and worry means that you will lead a productive and satisfying life.

Option 5: This answer is incorrect. Nothing can ensure life satisfaction and happiness, but managing emotions can help you reach this goal.

Option 6: This answer is correct. Becoming emotionally intelligent gives you the ability to cultivate appropriate emotional responses in a variety of settings.

In this lesson, "Managing Emotions," you will gain an understanding of the value and necessity of achieving emotional balance. You'll explore the following areas:
- knowing yourself,
- analyzing anger,
- dealing with anxiety and worry.

Imagine for a moment that you're trapped with several other people in the elevator of a 50-story skyscraper. The alarm is bellowing as the elevator occasionally jerks or bounces, unsettling its passengers.

What would be your most likely response to the situation just described? Would you:
- frantically begin searching the elevator for possible escape routes
- possibly read a book or engage in a conversation with another passenger while waiting for help
- thoroughly read the safety instructions posted in the elevator or provided by the emergency phone?

Your response to intense emotional experiences identifies your preferred emotional stance to stress and duress. In this segment, you'll explore the three distinctive styles people use for dealing with their emotions:
- feeling engulfed
- being accepting
- being self-aware

People who are engulfed by their emotions often feel like they have no control over their moods. They let their emotions "run wild" and are prone to overreacting and thinking the worst.

People engulfed by their emotions are the ones "freaking out," frantically searching for an escape from a stuck elevator before evaluating options.

Individuals accepting of their emotions do little to change how they feel. These people are aware of their feelings, but don't believe they can, or aren't willing to do anything about them.

See each type of individuals who are accepting of their emotions for more information.

Type 1

One type of "acceptor" is the person who's always in a good mood and, therefore, has no need or motivation to change.

Type 2

The other type is the person who is always in a bad mood, accepts it, and does nothing about it-- for example, reading a book during a crisis.

The third style of dealing with emotions is to be self-aware. Individuals who are self-aware have conscious thoughts about their moods as they experience them. There's a difference, for example, between acting frustrated with someone and just thinking, "I'm really feeling frustrated." When trapped in an elevator, the self-aware person recognizes his fear and begins to explore the options available.

See each aspect to learn more about the characteristic of self-aware people.

Step back

Being self-aware is a basic emotional competency which allows individuals to step back from an experience and observe what's happening, as opposed to being totally immersed in it.

Gain control

Self-awareness is the first step in gaining some control. You're not only aware of your mood, but also aware of your thought about that mood. When self-aware people are in a bad mood, they're able to get out of it sooner.

Positive outlook

Self-aware individuals are clear about their emotions and tend to be clear about their own boundaries. This leads to good psychological health and an overall positive outlook on life.

Thoughts

Although self-awareness can be a strictly nonjudgmental observation, it is often accompanied by thoughts like, "I wish I didn't feel this way," or, "I shouldn't be feeling this way."

Recognize feelings

While there is a difference between recognizing feelings and being aware of them, these two elements actually work together. To recognize you're feeling depressed signifies that you're wanting to feel happier.

Case Study: Question 1 of 2

Scenario

Antonio Damasio, a neurologist, provides an interesting example regarding emotional self-awareness. A patient who had a brain tumor removed subsequently suffered a dramatic personality change. While he was able to think logically, he was not capable of assigning value to a set of choices. The surgery this man had undergone severed the connection between his amygdala and his neocortex. As a result, he lacked awareness of his feelings. Although he could still process ideas logically, he was unable to make any decisions. He simply did not feel strongly enough about anything to make a decision one way or another.

Find out what bars the patient from making a decision by answering the questions.

Question

Why was Dr. Damasio's patient unable to make any decisions?

Options:

1. He was unable to think logically.

2. The link between his emotional and rational mind had been severed.

3. He was engulfed in his emotions and powerless to change them.

4. The motivation to feel had been eliminated.

Answer:

Actually, his rational mind (neocortex) was working; however, the connection to his emotional mind (amygdala) had been severed.

Option 1: This answer is incorrect. Dr. Damasio's patient was able to think logically, but he was incapable of assigning value to his choices.

Option 2: This is the correct answer. Dr. Damasio's patient was unable to make any decisions because his rational mind, the neocortex, was working; however, the connection to his emotional mind, the amygdala, had been severed.

Option 3: Incorrect. There was no indication that Dr. Damasio's patient was engulfed in his emotions, in fact he lacked any awareness of his feelings.

Option 4: This answer is incorrect. The patient's motivation to feel was unchanged, but he had no awareness of his emotions. Because of the surgery, he did not feel strongly enough about anything to make a decision one way or another.

Case Study: Question 2 of 2

When taken to extremes, emotional awareness can be troubling. Which extreme did Dr. Damasio's patient suffer from?

Options:

1. completely engulfed
2. lacking self-awareness

Answer:

Actually, Dr. Damasio's patient lacked any awareness of how he "felt" about anything.

Option 1: This answer is incorrect. If Dr. Damasio's patient was completely engulfed, he would have been aware of more feelings than he could deal with, rather than aware of none.

Option 2: This answer is correct. Dr. Damasio's patient suffered from lack of self-awareness because he lacked awareness of how he felt about anything.

Question

Three distinctive styles for handling emotions have been discussed.

Match each style with one or more corresponding behaviors.

Options:

A. engulfed
B. accepting
C. self-aware

Targets:

1. being clear about feelings but not trying to change them
2. having the ability to get out of a bad mood
3. feeling overwhelmed and out of control
4. doing nothing about good or bad moods
5. being clear about your own boundaries

Answer:

Actually, engulfed individuals are the ones who tend to "freak out;" accepting people don't do much about feelings; and self-aware individuals closely monitor their feelings.

When someone is accepting, they are clear about feelings but try not to change them because they don't believe they can, or aren't willing to do anything about them.

Someone who is self-aware has the ability to get out of a bad mood because not only are they aware of their mood, but they are also aware of their thoughts about that mood.

When someone is engulfed, they feel overwhelmed and out of control. They let their emotions "run wild" and are prone to overreacting and thinking the worst.

People who are accepting do nothing about good or bad moods because they have no need or motivation to change.

Someone who is self-aware is clear about their own boundaries as well as their emotions, which leads to good psychological health and an overall positive outlook on life.

There are varying degrees of self-awareness. As you just learned, when taken to extremes, emotional awareness can be troubling. For some people, awareness is overwhelming; for others, it barely exists. People who are overly tuned in to their emotions can increase the intensity and severity of their reactions to stressful situations and easily become engulfed.

People who use distraction to avoid tuning in to their emotions tend to be less aware of how they react to stressful situations. Therefore, their experiences tend to be less significant. However, some degree of emotional self-awareness is crucial to emotional intelligence.

Joe arrived home after a hard day. First his boss had blamed him for letting an important project fall behind schedule. Then he called his wife to check on the furnace repair and discovered she had forgotten the appointment, so the furnace didn't get fixed. On his way home, a driver cut him off, almost causing an accident. As he walked in the door, his son asked him for money to buy a new hat because he lost his old one. Joe yelled, "No way. You never take care of anything."

Joe let his anger get the best of him. It fueled actions he soon regretted. Many people have trouble curbing their anger. In fact, anger is the mood people have the hardest time controlling. In this segment, you'll learn:

- the physiological responses to anger,
- how physiological responses fuel escalation,
- common misconceptions about anger,
- how to defuse anger.

Anger creates a dual response in the body with short-term but lasting effects. The initial reaction is the "fight or flight" syndrome--the body senses a threat and prepares itself for possible attack. At the same time, the brain sends a signal that heightens sensitivity to subsequent events.

See each physiological response to anger for details.

A rush of energy

When angry feelings are triggered, the brain sends a rush of energy throughout the body. This surge lasts several minutes while the brain assesses the situation.

General alert

Meanwhile, the nervous system is put on general alert-- a state of readiness that lasts for hours or even days.

This persistent state of arousal explains why people get angry more quickly if they have already been provoked. The nervous system remains ready for any subsequent threats. Thus, anger builds on anger.

Contrary to popular belief, venting anger does little or nothing to dissipate it. Actually, venting is one of the worst ways to cool off after an outburst. It fuels the brain's emotional arousal and leaves people feeling more angry, not less.

Question

How long does the "fight or flight" syndrome last?

Options:

1. several minutes
2. several hours

Answer:

Actually, the "fight or flight" syndrome lasts several minutes, while the nervous system general alert lasts several hours or longer.

Option 1: This answer is correct. The "fight or flight" syndrome lasts several minutes because it is the immediate sense of a threat in which the body prepares itself for possible attack.

Option 2: This answer is incorrect. The immediate "fight or flight" response does not last several hours, but the nervous system's concurrent state of readiness may last for hours or even days.

There are three types of intervention that can lessen or eliminate anger. In fact, any angry mood can be sidestepped altogether if caught in its earliest stage. For example, Marvin has just blown up at his boss. As his anger escalated, it became more difficult for him to defuse it. He couldn't think straight and was oblivious to the consequences of any actions he might take.

Review each suggestion to learn how Marvin can calm himself.

Challenge the thoughts

One way to defuse anger is to challenge the thoughts that spark it. This is most effective when undertaken at early or moderate levels of anger. Once enraged, a person is no longer capable of rational thought--only of revenge and reprisal.

Distraction

Distraction can be useful for diminishing an angry mood. TV, movies, or reading can take your mind off the hostile thoughts. But shopping or eating may worsen anger by allowing you to dwell on the triggering situation.

Physical activity

You can deflate anger by engaging in a physical activity, especially by yourself. Deep breathing and relaxation exercises are also effective.

Question

The ability to deal with angry feelings appropriately hinges on understanding the physiological elements behind anger. Which statements describe what happens when someone is angry?

Options:

1. When someone is angry, anger builds on itself and is fueled by venting it.

2. When someone is angry, frustration builds until it is released by yelling at someone.

3. The brain generates two different physiological responses when someone is angry.

4. Once someone becomes angry, there is little that can be done to calm down--nature must take its course.

5. Watching TV or movies can de-escalate intense feelings that result when someone becomes angry.

Answer:

Remember, when someone becomes angry, strong physiological responses occur. These can be offset by challenging thoughts, physical activity, or distraction.

Option 1: This answer is correct. One of the physiological elements behind anger is that anger builds on itself. It fuels the brain's emotional arousal, which leaves people feeling angrier, not less angry.

Option 2: This answer is incorrect. Venting anger does not help to dispel it because it fuels the brain's emotional arousal and leaves people feeling angrier.

Option 3: This answer is correct. The two different physiological responses when someone is angry are the immediate surge and the lasting response.

Option 4: This answer is incorrect. It is not true that there is little that can be done to calm down anger. Three types of intervention that lessen anger are distraction, cooling off, and challenging the angry thoughts.

Option 5: This answer is correct. When you are angry, TV or movies can de-escalate intense feelings that result, because they can take your mind off the hostile thoughts.

Anger causes many people to behave in ways they later regret. They let their angry feelings overtake rational thought and escalate out of control. Understanding the body's response to anger can help curb it. In this segment, you learned:

- the physiological responses to anger,
- how physiological responses fuel escalation,
- common misconceptions about anger,
- how to defuse anger.

"Oh my gosh. I think I left my computer on at work. Dana has told me repeatedly to shut down my computer at the end of the day. I hope the system doesn't overload and cause a short. That will wipe out everything, and I'll lose my job. I'll have to live with my in-laws and work at a burger stand."

Does this sound familiar? You're not alone if at some point your mind has obsessed and fixated on a minor issue, making a mountain out of a molehill.

Although the perception of worry has traditionally been quite negative, not all worry is bad. Worrying can assist you in reflecting upon and developing positive solutions to problems. On the other hand, chronic worry creates a cycle of anxiety and unproductive obsessive thoughts. In this topic, you'll learn:

- the difference between worry and anxiety,
- the positive effects of worry,
- the negative effects of anxiety,
- techniques for minimizing anxiety.

Worry and anxiety are two points on a continuum. When a troublesome thought triggers the emotional brain, worry kicks in. Initially, this may generate constructive reflection. However, further down the continuum, it becomes chronic.

See each reaction for information on what happens to Pete, a sales manager, when he is worried or anxious.

Worry

When Pete is worried, his worry functions as a rehearsal for what may go wrong and provides a risk-free opportunity to evaluate solutions.

Anxiety

When Pete is anxious, his anxiety produces tunnel vision, causing him to obsess on a single negative outcome for the problem at hand.

Worry can serve a very useful purpose. Some of the aspects of worry that at first seem negative can actually produce positive results. Worries usually escalate from thought to thought within seconds. These thoughts are a steady progression of verbal expressions of concern, but seldom include images.

See each unexpected benefit of worry to learn more.

dealing with threats

When danger is sensed, worry allows you to assess your options, rehearse methods for dealing with them, and reflect upon desired outcomes.

catastrophizing

Catastrophizing is the process of imagining a worst-case scenario; it produces a series of terrible thoughts without a visual component. Because catastrophizing is expressed only as thoughts, not images, it does not leave a lasting impression.

suppressing anxiety

Worry can suppress the physiological effects of anxiety. When faced with anxiety, an individual launches into a train of distressing thoughts. Meanwhile, anxious sensations, like a racing heartbeat, can be lessened because the mind is distracted from the original triggering thought.

While worrying can have some positive effects, anxiety is a strictly negative experience. Anxiety focuses attention solely on the issue at hand and moves the mind to obsessing. This leads to an endless cycle with no hope of resolution, causing inflexibility and unrealistic perceptions.

Review each characteristic for more information about anxiety.

Physiological reactions

Anxiety causes physiological reactions such as sweating, a racing heart, and muscle tension.

Limits creative solutions

Anxiety prevents a worried person from shifting his mind away from his worries. This limits an individual's ability to develop creative solutions.

Ruminate on danger

Anxiety causes an individual to ruminate on dangers of all kinds--even things that have no chance of happening. These people see trouble at every corner.

Addicted to anxiety

Some people can become addicted to anxiety. If a person chronically worries about problems that rarely happen, he may attribute their nonoccurrence to his obsessing about them.

Self-awareness

Research has shown that the first step in minimizing anxiety is self-awareness. This means training yourself to identify situations that trigger worry, images that prompt worry, and sensations that signal anxiety in the body.

Challenge troubling thoughts

Once aware of anxious thoughts, the next step in eliminating anxiety is to actively challenge troubling thoughts. This involves questioning assumptions and maintaining a healthy skepticism toward the probability of occurrence.

Question

Worry and anxiety affect the emotions very differently. Match each emotional state with one or more of its corresponding effects.

Options:

A. worry
B. anxiety

Targets:

1. racing heart, sweating, and shakiness
2. inflexibility and narrow-minded thinking
3. rehearsing dangers and methods of dealing with them
4. coming up with solutions to potential problems
5. focusing on distressing thoughts without solutions

Answer:

It's important to remember that worry can actually produce some positive results, while anxiety leads to distress and narrow-minded thinking.

An effect of anxiety is a racing heart, sweating, and shakiness, which is an unhealthy physiological reaction.

An effect of anxiety is inflexibility and narrow-minded thinking which leads to an endless cycle with no hope of resolution.

An example of worry is rehearsing dangers and methods of dealing with them. Worry generates constructive reflection.

An example of worry is coming up with solutions to potential problems. Worry provides a risk-free opportunity to evaluate solutions.

An effect of anxiety is focusing on distressing thoughts without solutions, which limits an individual's ability to develop creative solutions.

Question

Which statements identify the emotional effects of anxiety and worry?

Options:

1. Anxiety is self-reinforcing.
2. Anxiety fixates attention on the threat at hand.
3. Worry causes shakiness and sweating.
4. Worry prevents "catastrophizing."
5. Positive outcomes are frequently attributed to chronic worry.

Answer:

Worry can have positive effects, while the effects of anxiety are negative.

Option 1: This answer is correct. Anxiety is self-reinforcing because if a person chronically worries about problems that rarely happen, he may attribute their nonoccurrence to his obsessing about them.

Option 2: This answer is correct. Anxiety fixates attention on the threat at hand. This can become problematic because it moves the mind to obsessing, which leads to an endless cycle with no hope of resolution.

Option 3: This answer is incorrect. Anxiety, not worry, causes shakiness and sweating.

Option 4: This answer is incorrect. Rather than preventing it, worry will lead to catastrophizing and produces a series of terrible thoughts without a visual component.

Option 5: This answer is correct. Because worry functions as a rehearsal for what may go wrong and provides a risk-free opportunity to evaluate solutions, positive outcomes are frequently attributed to chronic worry.

THE IMPACT OF EMOTIONAL INTELLIGENCE

The Impact of Emotional Intelligence

Have you ever been so stressed about taking a test that you felt like you just couldn't think? Conversely, have you ever been so enthusiastic and confident in pursuing a goal that nothing could have stopped you from succeeding?

The situations just described are two sides of the same coin, and they demonstrate how emotions can either get in the way of the ability to think or how they can actually enhance the ability to think.

Either way, your emotions set the limits of your capability to tap into your natural abilities.

Question

Being emotionally competent is more than just being in touch with your feelings. Actually, emotional intelligence has a far greater impact on life than that. Which statements are accurate with respect to the importance of being emotionally competent?

Options:

1. Being emotionally competent ensures personal and professional success.
2. Being emotionally competent enhances an individual's ability to make personal connections.
3. Being emotionally competent contributes to IQ scores and IQ-related achievements.
4. Being emotionally competent fosters the ability to use empathy.

Answer:

Actually, being emotionally competent enhances an individual's ability to make personal connections and use empathy. It does not contribute to IQ scores or guarantee personal and professional success.

Option 1: This answer is incorrect. Nothing can ensure personal and professional success, but being emotionally competent can enhance your probability for success.

Option 2: This answer is correct. Being emotionally competent enhances the ability to make personal connections because people who are strong at connecting recognize and respond appropriately to other people's feelings and concerns.

Option 3: This answer is incorrect. Being emotionally competent cannot contribute to IQ scores and achievements because these abilities are inherent and stable across time, and not related to emotional ability.

Option 4: This answer is correct. Being emotionally competent fosters the ability to use empathy. Individuals with high levels of empathy are more sensitive and better adjusted emotionally.

In this lesson, "The Impact of Emotional Intelligence," you'll explore how emotions affect so many areas of your life by learning about the following:

- the characteristics of emotional intelligence,
- the importance of emotional intelligence,
- how social skills are affected by emotional intelligence.

Psychologist Walter Mischel started some interesting research in 1960. Working with 4-year-old children at the preschool on the Stanford University campus, he used an interesting model to evaluate the importance of emotional intelligence. The children were promised two marshmallows as a treat if they could wait until someone returned from an errand. If the child couldn't wait until then, the child could have only one--but could have it immediately.

The choice made by these children became a telling tale about emotional intelligence and about one of the basic characteristics associated with emotional intelligence--impulse control.

Impulse control is just one of the several characteristics that predict and measure emotional intelligence. The other characteristics that contribute to emotional intelligence are:
- mood manipulation
- hope
- optimism

Impulse control is often considered the core of emotional self-management. This is probably because emotions by nature call for action or response. That's why Walter Mischel's research is so interesting. For up to 20 minutes, some 4-year-olds hid their eyes, sang, played games, and talked to themselves while waiting for the two-marshmallow reward. However, other children took the one marshmallow almost immediately after the facilitator left the room.

See each aspect for more information about impulse control.

behavioral differences

When researchers followed up on Mischel's test group 14 years later, there was a marked difference between the group that took the marshmallow and the group that was able to delay gratification.

temptation

The children who had been able to control their impulses at 4 years old were found to be more socially competent adolescents. These children were also more self-assertive and demonstrated more competence in handling frustration, stress, and pressure.

challenge

Mischel's research found that the group of children with gratification-delay ability were better able to face challenges and were more likely to be relentless in their pursuit of valued goals. The children without impulse control were more easily upset and put off by frustrations.

personal traits

The 4-year-olds who resisted the treat displayed more personal integrity than those who couldn't wait. Qualities like trustworthiness, dependability, and self-reliance were evident in these individuals. The marshmallow-grabbing group had fewer of these qualities.

lifelong predictor

Impulse control is a strong predictor of lifelong success, signifying the ability to identify situations in which delay and resisting temptation would be beneficial in achieving goals.

mental ability

Walter Mischel's research proved that the ability to control impulses when focusing on a goal is the essence of emotional competency. His findings clearly identify emotional intelligence as a critical factor in using other mental abilities to the greatest capacity.

Question

Walter Mischel's marshmallow test identified several behaviors that are associated with impulse control. Which traits correspond with Mischel's findings?

Options:

1. ability to face challenges
2. social competence
3. self-assertiveness
4. aggression
5. forcefulness
6. trustworthiness

Answer:

The correct answers identify the behaviors that correspond to Mischel's findings.

Option 1: This answer is correct. One behavior associated with impulse control is the ability to face challenges, because individuals are more likely to be relentless in their pursuit of valued goals.

Option 2: Correct. A behavior associated with impulse control is social competence. Individuals with impulse control are better able to handle different personality types because they have more patience.

Option 3: This answer is correct. Individuals who show impulse control are also self-assertive and demonstrate more competence in handling frustration, stress, and pressure.

Option 4: This answer is incorrect. Aggression in itself is impulsive, so it would not be a behavior associated with impulse control.

Option 5: This answer is incorrect. Forcefulness has a negative connotation and would not be considered a behavior associated with impulse control.

Option 6: This answer is correct. A behavior associated with impulse control is trustworthiness because dependability and self-reliance are evident in trustworthy individuals.

The second characteristic that contributes to emotional competence is mood manipulation. Even small mood changes can color a person's ability to think clearly.

See each person for more information on how moods affect their thinking.

Person 1

"Good moods actually enhance my ability to think and problem solve. Laughing frees up my creativity and promotes my ability to see complex relationships and consequences. Joking can actually help me think through a problem."

Person 2

"Studies show that problems are more likely to be solved by someone who's just had a good laugh. After watching a show about television bloopers, I was better able to find alternative solutions to a problem that was weighing heavily on my mind."

Person 3

"When making important decisions, I prefer to be in a good mood. It helps me think more positively and comprehensively. I consider the pros and cons, recall positive events, and am more likely to make a sound decision when I'm "up.""

Person 4

"When I'm in a bad mood and try to make decisions, I can only recall the negative. I find that I'm overly cautious, and my emotions cause me to make decisions based on my fear."

The other two characteristics that contribute to emotional intelligence are hope and optimism. Recent research shows that hope is a crucial element in a vast array of abilities. In everything from taking tests to handling a difficult boss, hope is more than just a vague belief. It has been discovered that hope gives people confidence that they have the will and the means to achieve their goals. In terms of emotional intelligence, hope plays a role in not giving into defeat, depression, setbacks, or anxiety. People with hope have less emotional stress.

Optimism is an extension of hope. If hope is not giving into defeat, depression, setbacks, or anxiety, then optimism is the attitude that goes along with it.

- Optimism protects people from apathy and depression.
- Optimistic people see failure as an event that they can overcome.
- Optimism prevents people from blaming their failures on personal traits which they cannot change.

Martin Seligman's study of insurance salesmen is perhaps one of the greatest examples of the power of optimism. Seligman discovered that new salesmen who were naturally optimistic sold 37 percent more than individuals who where pessimistic. The difference was attributed to what happened when rejected.

The pessimistic salesman interprets "no," personally--"I'm a failure." The optimistic one interprets "no" quite differently--"I need to try a new approach."

Question

Here are various emotional characteristics. Identify all those that contribute to emotional competency.

Options:

1. hope and optimism
2. masking and denial
3. mood manipulation
4. impulse control

Answer:

Actually, hope, optimism, mood manipulation, and impulse control are emotional characteristics that contribute to emotional competency.

Option 1: Correct. Hope and optimism contribute to emotional competence, because hope gives people confidence that they have the will and the means to achieve their goals. And optimism is an extension of hope.

Option 2: This answer is incorrect. Masking and denial take away from emotional competency by covering up or placing blame.

Option 3: Correct. Mood manipulation contributes to emotional competence because even small mood changes can color a person's ability to think clearly. A positive attitude and good mood enhance the ability to think and problem solve.

Option 4: Correct. Impulse control contributes to emotional competence and is often considered the core of emotional self-management, since emotions by nature call for action or response.

Research has shown that there are several characteristics that contribute to emotional intelligence:
- impulse control,
- mood manipulation,
- hope and optimism.

A group of young children is playing together. Sally sees another girl crying and goes over to comfort her. She pats her hair and gives her a small toy to play with. Meanwhile, Jimmy yanks a toy from his playmate and gleefully displays it over his head. While his playmate cries, Jimmy teases him--"Ha, ha, I've got your truck." Now fast-forward 25 years: Who is more popular? Outgoing? Sensitive?

Sally's ability to empathize, apparent even at a young age, contributes to her emotional intelligence. The benefits of showing empathy include being better adjusted emotionally, more popular, more outgoing, and more sensitive. In this segment, you will learn:
- the origins of empathy in children,
- the physiological basis for empathy,
- how empathy is conveyed through nonverbal messages,
- the consequences when empathy is absent.

Empathy is the ability to sense another's emotional state and, as in Sally's case, is often visible at an early age. Studies show that parents can foster empathy in children by using discipline that points out how their misbehavior causes someone else to feel, rather than emphasizing the "badness" of the behavior. Empathy can be stifled when attunement between parents and children is absent--when parents consistently ignore their children's feelings.

Children whose emotions have been ignored begin to avoid expressing emotions and may even stop feeling emotions. With awareness of their own feelings blunted, they lose the ability to empathize because understanding others' feelings is impossible without sensing your own first.

Studies have found evidence that our brains are wired for empathy. Initial research in monkeys and subsequent research in humans leaves no doubt that empathy has a physiological basis.

See each aspect for more information on reading nonverbal expressions.

evidence in monkeys

Studies show that monkeys recognize emotional expressions in one another. Examination of monkeys' brains revealed activity in the visual cortex and amygdala when this empathy-type behavior occurred.

evidence in humans

Special neuron activity in the amygdala occurs when reading nonverbal expressions and gestures that communicate specific emotions and not, for example, merely when recognizing a familiar face.

when emotionally aroused

When emotionally aroused, such as experiencing strong anger, people are less able to read others' nonverbal signals because their own physiological responses (heart pounding, sweating, etc.) get in the way.

when calm and receptive

A person in a calm state is receptive and better able to read others' subtle nonverbal signals because her own physiological state doesn't interfere.

Research has shown that 90 percent or more of an emotional message is nonverbal. Recognizing common nonverbal cues enhances your ability to empathize with others. This is a skill that, in general, women are better at than men.

Read about each emotional state to learn how Jolene, a skilled human resource manager, reads nonverbal signals and messages.

Nervousness or embarrassment

"Hands or fingers in front of the mouth express nervousness or embarrassment."

Suspicion or rejection

"Rubbing the eyes can communicate suspicion or rejection--unconsciously saying, "I don't believe what I'm seeing.""

Disagreement or resentment

"Arms folded across the chest often indicate disagreement or resentment, especially when accompanied by sighing or rolling the eyes."

Helplessness

"Open hands, palms up, can send a message of helplessness or a plea to be understood."

Aggressiveness

"Pointing, especially with an implement such as a pen, can signify aggressiveness. This is often accompanied by intense eye contact."

Lack of interest

"Leaning back or away from the speaker communicates a lack of interest or pulling away from involvement."

Empathy and sympathy are distinct skills. Sympathy involves the ability to view a situation and sense what you yourself might feel, while empathy requires you to look at that situation and sense what the other person is feeling (it may not be the same as your feelings).

Review each characteristic for more information about psychopaths, personalities that are mentally disordered.

Incapable of empathy

Psychopathic personalities are generally incapable of empathy.

Absence of empathy

The absence of empathy gives psychopaths the ability to project feelings on their victims totally unlike what the victims are actually feeling.

Question

A key component of emotional intelligence is the ability to show empathy. Which statements describe empathy?

Options:

1. Empathy is the ability to sense another's emotional state.

2. The ability to empathize is based in the amygdala.

3. The absence of empathy is exhibited by increasing anger and rage.

4. The more articulate you are, the greater your ability to show empathy to another person.

5. Signs of empathy begin in infancy.

6. The degree to which one can empathize is instinctive and cannot be changed.

Answer:

Actually, the ability to sense another's emotional state is based in the amygdala and begins in infancy.

Option 1: This answer is correct. Empathy is the ability to sense another's emotional state and is often visible at an early age. It is a contributor to emotional intelligence.

Option 2: This answer is correct. The ability to empathize is based in the amygdala, and is apparent because activity in that part of the brain occurs when reading nonverbal expressions and gestures that communicate specific emotions.

Option 3: This answer is incorrect. The absence of empathy is characterized by the impairment of social interactions, not by increasing anger and rage.

Option 4: This answer is incorrect. Verbal skills will not assist someone in showing empathy. It's not what you say, but how you show that you understand what the other person is feeling that expresses true empathy.

Option 5: Correct. Signs of empathy begin in infancy. Parents can foster empathy in children by using discipline to point out how bad behavior makes others feel, or can stifle it by consistently ignoring their children's feelings.

Option 6: This answer is incorrect. While empathy can begin in infancy, it is a learned behavior and can be changed depending on parental interaction.

Emotional intelligence is enhanced by the ability to empathize, and when it is lacking, it can seriously impair social interactions. Individuals with high levels of empathy are more sensitive and better adjusted emotionally. In this segment, you learned:

- the origins of empathy in children,
- the physiological basis for empathy,
- how empathy is conveyed through nonverbal messages,
- the consequences when empathy is absent.

Lana was technically bright and possessed great career promise. However, she lacked simple social skills and grace. She was outgoing to the point of being bold. She tended to snicker and laugh at inopportune moments. She cracked inappropriate jokes that made people uncomfortable, and her overly friendly manner made many of her colleagues uneasy.

Lana's social ineptness and her inability to notice or handle the emotional responses of others caused emotional havoc wherever she went.

You might be thinking, "I know someone just like Lana--someone with an obvious lack of social grace and skill." People like Lana have the following traits in common.

- They are unable to read social cues from other people.
- They center conversations around themselves.
- They don't recognize subtle ways others use to end conversations.
- They are unable to follow the lead of others in deflecting uncomfortable questions.

Thomas Hatch and Howard Gardner's research on multiple intelligence identifies four social skills that contribute to and enhance emotional intelligence, working to combat the ineptitudes just described. The four social skills are as follows:

- organizing groups,
- negotiating solutions,
- making personal connections,
- performing social analyses.

Being capable of organizing groups is a significant skill for emotionally intelligent people. This skill revolves around the ability to initiate and coordinate the efforts of various people toward common goals.

See each person for more information on how they demonstrate skill in organizing groups.

Kate

Kate has the ability to relate to people from various backgrounds and pay close attention to what motivates people.

Cheryl

Cheryl has basic leadership skills. She has a vision and is capable of offering direction comfortably.

Individuals who are able to negotiate have a unique talent for mediating. Not only can these individuals resolve conflicts when they occur, but in many cases, they are capable of keeping the lid on trouble when it's brewing.

People who are skilled at negotiation focus on solutions and actions, rather than problems and roadblocks.

Some people seem to naturally sense and relate to other people's feelings. These people, who are skilled in making personal connections, recognize and respond in appropriate ways to the feelings and concerns of others.

See each skill of personal connection for more information.

using empathy

The ability to use empathy effectively makes it easy for an individual to enter into a conversation or social setting.

connecting

People who are strong at connecting recognize and respond appropriately to other people's feelings and concerns.

participating

Individuals who are skilled at making personal connections automatically participate with others. They make great team players and business partners.

reading emotions

People who are skilled in making connections get along well with virtually everyone because they are so quick to read the emotional climate. This skill helps them succeed as sales people, managers, and teachers.

In addition to organizing groups, negotiating solutions, and forming personal connections, individuals who possess social skills that contribute to their emotional intelligence have one final skill: social analysis.

See each aspect for more information about social analysis.

Knowing how other people are feeling

Social analysis is the skill of knowing and understanding how other people are feeling. This can lead to easy intimacy or, at the very least, the ability to build rapport quickly.

Detect feelings

Social analysis is more than just talking to people. It means being able to detect feelings--to sense what's going on. This analysis offers insights about people's feelings, motives, and concerns.

Question

Match each of the social skills that enhance emotional intelligence with one or more corresponding behaviors.

Options:

A. organizing groups
B. negotiating solutions
C. personal connections
D. social analysis

Targets:
1. detecting other people's motives
2. handling situations with diplomacy
3. practicing the art of relationships
4. functioning with a strong sense of dependability
5. initiating movement of various people toward common goals

Answer:

Actually, individuals who possess emotional intelligence have the ability to organize people toward common goals, prevent conflict, build rapport, and detect underlying emotions.

Detecting other people's motives is key to social analysis because it allows you to sense what's going on. This analysis offers insights about people's feelings, motives, and concerns.

Being able to negotiate solutions means handling situations with diplomacy. These individuals focus on solutions and actions, rather than problems and roadblocks.

Practicing the art of relationships is important when making personal connections. These individuals recognize and respond appropriately to other people's feelings and concerns.

Functioning with a strong sense of dependability is a key to making personal connections. These people automatically participate with others, which makes them great team players and business partners.

Initiating movement of various people toward common goals is an example of organizing groups. Individuals with this skill relate to people from various backgrounds, pay close attention to what motivates people, and offer direction comfortably.

People who make an excellent social impression possess a high degree of emotional intelligence. In addition to having an astute sense of their own needs and how to fulfill them, they are skilled in the following four areas:
- organizing groups,
- negotiating solutions,
- making personal connections,
- performing social analyses.

BECOMING EMOTIONALLY LITERATE

Becoming Emotionally Literate

The media are full of troubling stories. One identifies guns as the number one cause of death in America. One says that murder rates rose by 3 percent. Yet another shows an increase in violent crimes. Where are we headed?

While the statistics are scary, there is hope. Many problems we are now facing can be prevented or controlled through emotional literacy.

Question

While some people believe that emotional literacy is a passing fad, there's reason to believe that it has a long-range and significant impact on society as a whole. Which statements identify the importance of being emotionally literate?

Options:

1. Emotional literacy will soon replace IQ.
2. Emotional literacy affects both individuals and society as a whole.

3. Most of society's problems could be solved through an increase in emotional literacy.

4. Aggression can be tamed by increasing emotional literacy.

Answer:

Actually, emotional literacy has a tremendous impact on individuals and society. While it can't solve all of society's problems, it can be used to help with issues like aggression.

Option 1: This answer is incorrect. Emotional literacy will never replace IQ, but it will enhance our ability to relate to one another.

Option 2: This answer is correct. Emotional literacy affects individuals and the society. Many problems we are now facing can be helped by increased emotional literacy.

Option 3: This answer is incorrect. Emotional literacy can't solve all of society's problems, but it can be used to help with issues like anger, aggression, and violence.

Option 4: This answer is correct. Aggression can be tamed by increasing emotional literacy because the more we understand the connection between the two, the more likely we will be to foster emotional literacy at a young age.

As you can see, the impact of emotional literacy is significant. In this lesson, you'll gain an understanding of:
- temperament and emotional literacy,
- the need for emotional literacy,
- educating the emotions.

As all parents can attest, every baby is different. Some are naturally easy and seldom cry, while others are easily upset. These early indications of temperament often stick for life, and the easy babies become sociable, popular adults, while the timid babies grow into shy and anxious adults. Why is this? Is temperament destiny? Is emotional literacy (or illiteracy) determined from birth?

Genetics do affect emotional literacy. Every individual is "hard wired" with a genetic predisposition for a certain temperament. However, while temperament has a biological basis, it can be altered. This segment will explain:

- basic temperaments and their characteristics,
- specific brain functions and their effects on temperament,
- how innate predispositions can be molded through experience.

Studies of children from infancy through young adulthood have found that those babies who are most timid and fearful tend to retain anxious and timid temperaments into adulthood, while babies who are bold and relaxed tend to become sociable, confident, and popular adults.

See each aspect for more information on how genetics influence temperament.

genetic response to stress

Timid babies exhibit greater reactions to stress than bold babies; their hearts beat faster when faced with strange situations. They treat any new person or circumstance as a threat.

amygdala activity and temperament

The amygdala of a timid baby is more easily aroused than that of a bold baby; the nervous system activates the amygdala more quickly. On the other hand, the amygdala of an outgoing baby is less excitable; the nervous system has a higher threshold before activating the amygdala.

parental influence on temperament

Parents can moderate a timid baby's fearfulness by setting firm limits and insisting on obedience. Parents who are lenient and indirect with timid babies tend to reinforce their fearfulness, making it more difficult for them to become outgoing adults.

Humans are primed by genetics to respond to situations in either a generally positive or generally negative way. Brain wave patterns can classify people as tending toward a morose or upbeat temperament. Becky, a parent of twin girls, can attest to these differences in her two children.

See each of the twins to reveal how their temperaments differ.

Anna

Anna has a cheerful temperament and the ability to bounce back from setbacks. This is due to greater activity in the left frontal lobe.

Emma

Emma has a tendency toward melancholy and negativity. This is due to higher levels of activity in the right frontal lobe.

Emotional experiences can actually change the neural circuitry in the brain, affecting ingrained temperament. For example, Sandy's son Ryan was fearful of water. Sandy helped him overcome his fear by participating in swimming lessons with him. This gave Ryan's neural circuits a chance to build new pathways that superseded the existing ones, which held the fear of water.

Psychotherapy (emotional relearning) can accomplish the same thing and transcend ingrained temperaments by reshaping brain functions.

Question

Temperament and genetics are interconnected. Which statements accurately identify the ways genetics and temperament influence emotional intelligence?

Options:

1. Brain patterns affecting temperament are most easily changed in childhood.
2. Increased activity in the amygdala is associated with timidity and fearfulness.
3. Activity in the left frontal lobe is an indicator of a pessimistic or melancholy temperament.
4. Social competence is ingrained at an early age and cannot change.

Answer:

You have not identified how genetics and temperament influence emotional literacy.

Option 1: This answer is correct. Brain patterns are most easily changed in childhood because they have had less opportunity to become ingrained.

Option 2: This answer is correct. The amygdala of a timid baby is more easily aroused than that of a bold baby because the nervous system activates the amygdala more quickly.

Option 3: This answer is incorrect. Activity in the left frontal lobe indicates a cheerful temperament and the ability to bounce back from setbacks.

Option 4: This answer is incorrect. While social competence is present at an early age, it can be changed through emotional relearning.

Genetics and temperament influence emotional literacy. Temperament has a biological basis; however, it can be shaped through emotional experiences and the following:

- individual characteristics of temperament,
- how specific brain functions affect temperament,
- how experience "rewires" innate predispositions.

Phillip had been fired from his position with the accounting firm where he'd worked for over 12 years. Though he was known for being somewhat different, Phillip's behavior on this particular day shocked everyone. Returning to the office armed with an automatic weapon, he began firing rounds.

Two of Phillip's co-workers died, and he took his own life before the ordeal ended.

Acts like Phillip's are glaring examples of a society that has an alarming deficiency in emotional intelligence. In this segment, you'll learn about the specific problems that may result from emotional illiteracy.

- withdrawal or social problems,
- depression,
- attention or thinking problems,
- aggressive behavior.

Withdrawal is probably the most common social problem that results from a lack of emotional intelligence. While everyone needs a certain amount of "alone time," people who are severely lacking in emotional intelligence take this idea to the extreme. Follow along as Beverly explains how this problem affected her.

I started off just preferring to be alone, but after a while, I wasn't able to function normally when surrounded by other people. I found them bothersome, as opposed to enjoying the interaction.

Next, I noticed that I didn't want to tell anyone anything. I was overly secretive, and I felt I couldn't trust anyone. Consequently, I had trouble developing relationships.

As a result of having no connections and being withdrawn, I began to sulk a lot. I was really feeling sorry for myself.

Then, I had an overall drop in energy. I was never "up." I constantly complained of being tired or overwhelmed.

Feeling unhappy became an acceptable state for me. Since I spent so little time with other people, I began to lose my perspective and viewed life with a self-imposed negative bias.

Finally, I found myself overly dependent upon drugs and alcohol, which only served to make me more withdrawn.

I'm going to send you an article on Netiquette to help you learn more. Let's get back to business for now.

Although there are many causes for depression, including biochemical imbalances, depression may also be caused by emotional illiteracy. Roger suffers from depression and experiences the following:

- being lonely,
- having many fears and worries,
- needing to be perfect,
- feeling unloved,
- feeling nervous,
- being sad.

The third type of problem that may result from emotional illiteracy revolves around attention or thinking problems. These problems often display themselves through nervous or overly active behavior.

See each person for more information on how attention or thinking problems affected them.

Jeremy
"I find it difficult to sit still and very often feel too nervous to concentrate or get my mind focused on the issues at hand."

Felicia
"I find myself daydreaming constantly. I have difficulty getting my mind off a topic, and I often act without thinking.

Question
So far, you've explored three specific problems that may result from emotional illiteracy. Match each behavior with one or more resultant emotional illiteracy problems.

Options:
A. withdrawal
B. depression
C. attention or thinking problems

Targets:
1. feeling unloved
2. finding it difficult to sit still
3. being overly secretive
4. daydreaming
5. having low energy

Answer:
The correct answers match the behaviors with the problems resulting from a lack of emotional intelligence.

Depression can cause sensations of feeling unloved, as well as being lonely, feeling nervous and sad.

People with attention or thinking problems may find it difficult to sit still. Because of this over-active behavior, individuals often feel too nervous to concentrate or get their mind focused on the issues at hand.

Withdrawal causes being overly secretive and makes developing relationships troublesome.

People with attention or thinking problems may find themselves daydreaming. They may also have difficulty getting their mind off a topic, and often act without thinking.

Withdrawal causes low energy because of the lack of interaction as well as being tired or overwhelmed.

While withdrawal is probably the most common social problem that may be caused by emotional illiteracy, aggression is likely the most troublesome.

See each aspect for more information on aggression.

Neutral acts appear to be threats

Aggressive behavior is based on a perceptual bias that causes the individual to be highly sensitive to unfair treatment. Consequently, even neutral acts appear to be threats.

Jumping to judgment

Jumping to the judgment that most acts are hostile or threatening causes an individual to pay too little attention to what's really happening. Once that assumption is made, the person moves into action.

Low emotional tolerance

Aggressive individuals have low emotional tolerance, and get irritated more often by little things. Once upset, they see all acts as hostile and begin concentrating on how to strike back.

Perceptual biases toward hostility

Perceptual biases toward hostility are in place at an early age. Aggressive children are often rejected by their peers and are unable to make friends easily. These children are most at risk for eventually committing violent crimes.

Question

Emotional illiteracy is the cause of several problems. Which problems listed here, may be caused by emotional illiteracy?

Options:

1. alcoholism
2. withdrawal
3. aggression
4. depression
5. divorce

Answer:

Actually, withdrawal, depression, and aggression are all results of emotional illiteracy. Additionally, attention or thinking problems have been traced to a lack of emotional intelligence

Option 1: This answer is incorrect. Alcoholism may result from withdrawal, aggression, or depression but is not a direct result of emotional illiteracy.

Option 2: Correct. Emotional illiteracy causes withdrawal because people who are severely lacking in emotional intelligence take the idea of alone time to the extreme.

Option 3: Correct. Emotional illiteracy can cause aggression. Aggressive individuals have low emotional tolerance, and get irritated more often by little things.

Option 4: Correct. Depression may be caused by emotional illiteracy because individuals feel lonely, have fears and worries, need to be perfect, and feel unloved, nervous, and sad.

Option 5: Incorrect. Divorce may result from withdrawal, aggression, or depression but emotional illiteracy does not cause it directly.

Emotional illiteracy may cause a variety of problems for individuals and for society.

- withdrawal or social problems,
- depression,
- attention or thinking problems,
- aggressive behavior.

Do you know someone who is self-disciplined or who leads a virtuous life? Do you know someone who is able to motivate and guide himself personally and professionally? Do you know someone who has the ability to delay gratification and to control and channel his urges, will, appetites, and passions? Do you know someone who knows how to do right by himself and others?

If so, you know someone who possesses a somewhat old-fashioned trait called "character." Character is the essence of emotional intelligence.

How do you enable an individual--or yourself--to develop character? It's not enough to simply lecture people about educating their emotions. Rather, character is made up of the following skills.

- practicing emotional self-awareness,
- harnessing emotions productively,
- reading emotions in others.

Practicing emotional self-awareness is essential in educating the emotions and building character.

See each task for more information on how you can practice emotional self-awareness.

recognizing and naming emotions

This requires building a vocabulary for feelings so that when an emotion is experienced, you're able to label that emotion appropriately. For example, when you're passed over for a promotion, are you just angry? Chances are that you're more than angry--you're frustrated and hurt.

understanding the causes of feelings

Understanding causes of feelings means dedicating yourself to observing your own behavior and recognizing the feelings that various situations elicit. For example, when someone treats you with indifference, do you give up or try harder to get them to notice you?

recognizing the difference between feelings and actions

There's a big difference between thought and action. To become more emotionally self-aware, you must understand the relationship between your thoughts and reactions. When you examine your actions, pay attention to whether your thoughts or feelings are ruling.

Harnessing emotions requires monitoring self-talk to catch any internal negative messages. It also means taking time to understand what's behind your feelings and finding ways to handle fear, anxiety, anger, and sadness.

Follow along as Eduardo monitors his self-talk during a conversation with his boss, Buck, regarding being passed over for a promotion.

Eduardo: Buck, I'd appreciate some feedback on why I was passed over for that promotion last week.

Buck: Well, Eduardo, I felt Vivian was better qualified for the job.

Eduardo: (to himself) I'll bet she's better qualified, but not for work. I want to tell this jerk what I think about this decision. I don't care what happens...I'm so angry. But if I tell Buck how I feel right now, I may lose my job altogether, and I need a paycheck this week. I have to communicate my frustration in a more appropriate way.

Eduardo: What specific factors did you use when determining who was best qualified?

Buck: I looked at work experience, time with the organization, and input from supervisors and peers.

Eduardo: (to himself) I may not have been here as long as Vivian, but I know more than she does. No one gives me any respect around here, but I guess I'm going to have to prove myself in this organization.

Eduardo: That makes sense. I'm glad to know that longevity is a factor in getting promoted, because I plan on making my future with this company.

The third method that can be used to educate the emotions is reading emotions in others. This involves practice in taking another person's perspective.

See each statement for more information on how Shelly, a marketing executive, became skilled in reading emotions in others.

Shelly 1

"I really try to take the other person's perspective. I know that I must first appreciate the differences in how people feel about things."

Shelly 2

"I work on listening effectively and asking a lot of questions. Additionally, I try to work on recognizing my own reactions to what people say and do."

Question

There are many methods that can be used to educate emotions. Which methods listed here are valid?

Options:

1. learning to ignore emotional responses
2. improving self-awareness
3. using morality more effectively
4. harnessing emotions productively
5. reading emotions in others
6. improving logic and reasoning skills

Answer:

The correct answers show that improving self-awareness, harnessing emotions, and reading others' emotions with empathy will help educate your emotions.

Option 1: This answer is incorrect. Ignoring emotional responses will not help you understand them and in some cases will lessen their impact because you will never understand what's behind your feelings.

Option 2: Correct. One method that can be used to educate emotions is improving self awareness by labeling emotions, understanding the causes of feelings, and understanding the relationship between thoughts and reactions.

Option 3: This answer is incorrect. Using morality effectively is outside the scope of educating emotions because morality speaks to how you live your life rather than how you react emotionally.

Option 4: Correct. One method that can be used to educate emotions is to harness emotions productively through self-talk, which should catch any internal negative messages. It also means taking time to understand what is behind your feelings.

Option 5: Correct. One method that can be used to educate emotions is reading emotions in others, which involves practice in taking another person's perspective.

Option 6: This answer is incorrect. Logic and reasoning skills will not help you educate or more fully understand your emotions because logic and reasoning do not involve emotions.

It's not enough to simply lecture people about educating their emotions. Rather, character is made up of skills that must be practiced. To improve your emotional intelligence, remember to focus on:
- practicing emotional self-awareness,
- harnessing your emotions,
- reading emotions in others.

Being able to control the urge to focus solely on self and to control negative impulses offers a vast array of benefits to the individual and to society as a whole. These emotional intelligence skills open the path to empathy and listening, which in turn lead to caring and compassion. This dynamic combination breeds tolerance and acceptance of differences, increases mutual respect, and creates the possibility of fulfilling personal and professional relationships.

Becoming emotionally intelligent is the key.

CHAPTER II - EMOTIONAL INTELLIGENCE IN THE WORKPLACE

CHAPTER II - Emotional Intelligence in the Workplace

Studies show that emotional intelligence plays a role that's just as, if not more, important than IQ. By developing your people skills, you'll have a positive effect on your career.

In this course, you'll explore:

- what emotional intelligence is,
- how to realistically evaluate yourself,
- why it's important to manage your emotions,
- how self-motivation affects your career.

A DIFFERENT KIND OF SMART

A Different Kind of Smart

Is the smartest person always the most successful? Does the highest IQ predict the most success in life? Or are there other factors that help determine what we accomplish?

Success and ability aren't just factors of IQ. You probably know at least one person who got great grades in school, but hasn't built a strong career. Likewise, you know someone who struggled in school, but has built a rewarding work life. IQ is only one facet of intelligence. There is also another part of intelligence, called emotional intelligence. This type of brainpower refers to people's ability to relate to others and control emotions.

Question

Why is emotional intelligence important in the workplace?

Options:

1. If you have high emotional intelligence, you can build better relationships with your co-workers.

2. Emotional intelligence helps you make better decisions.

3. If you have high emotional intelligence, you reduce your need for technical knowledge.

4. Emotional intelligence helps you avoid unproductive conflict.

Answer:

Actually, emotional intelligence helps you understand others and build productive relationships. It can also help you avoid unproductive conflict and make better decisions.

Option 1: This answer is correct. Possessing emotional intelligence means you will build better relationships with your co-workers because you have empathy and other social skills.

Option 2: This answer is correct. Emotional intelligence helps you make better decisions because of your personal abilities, which include self-awareness, self-regulation, and motivation.

Option 3: This answer is incorrect. Just because you have emotional intelligence, it does not mean you do not need technical knowledge, especially if you are in a technical field.

Option 4: This answer is correct. Emotional intelligence helps you to avoid unproductive conflict, especially with co-workers and clients, because you know how to regulate your emotions.

In this lesson, you'll investigate some common misconceptions about intelligence. You'll explore a new definition of intelligence and learn some of the common characteristics of top performers.

You'll see why some typical ways of measuring intelligence aren't relevant in the workplace, and you'll see the competencies that affect workplace success.

Daniel was the smartest person in his college classes. His IQ was high, his grades were nearly perfect, and he had top scores on several standardized tests. Can Daniel expect a successful career? Will he perform better in the workplace than his classmates?

Question

Is the statement true or false?

Experts would predict that Daniel will have a successful career based on his IQ.

Options:

1. true
2. false

Answer:

IQ is not a reliable predictor of Daniel having a successful career.

Option 1: This statement is not true. While Daniel may very likely be successful, IQ is not an accurate predictor of career success.

Option 2: This statement is false. Career success cannot be predicted based on IQ alone because other qualities such as emotional effectiveness are important for success as well.

The idea that IQ predicts career success is one of the most common misconceptions about intelligence. In this topic, you'll learn more about why IQ is not an accurate predictor of career success.

You'll also explore some of the other, more common, misconceptions about intelligence.

It's common to believe that those with high IQs have an advantage. However, IQ is not always the most important factor in life and career success. Some common myths about intelligence are:
- Career success can be predicted based on IQ.
- The most successful companies hire the "smartest" employees.
- The best job candidate has the highest IQ.

Daniel and Eric completed the same graduate engineering program. Daniel's IQ is somewhat higher than Eric's and his grades were perfect. Eric's academic performance was only slightly higher than average.

See each engineer to reveal how their careers progressed.

Daniel
Daniel's work is flawless and he thoroughly understands technical issues. However, he hasn't been promoted during the five years he's been with the firm.

Eric
Eric has a good grasp of technical issues and he rarely makes mistakes. He's been promoted once and is looking forward to another move up the ladder next years.

Daniel may have a lot of intelligence, but he's missing some critical skills for success. Eric doesn't have the highest IQ, but he's smart enough to know how to work with people. Eric has high emotional intelligence. He's moved up in his career because he is pleasant to work with and he's able to motivate those around him to accomplish goals. Daniel's work is on time and perfect, but he makes his co-workers uncomfortable and he isn't an effective team member.

Career success can't be predicted based on IQ alone. While a certain IQ may be needed to enter a field like engineering, academic intelligence alone does not equal workplace achievement.

Another common misconception about intelligence is that successful companies hire the "smartest" employees.

Brenda has been the recruiting manager at a large, industry-leading computer company for the past 15 years. She's learned a lot about the skills successful employees need.

See each statement, in order, to learn about Brenda's recruiting experiences.

Statement 1

"I find that employees who had great grades in school aren't always the most successful at our company. We need people who have a wide range of skills that can't be measured by test scores or grades."

Statement 2

"We used to test applicants' intelligence using standardized tests. We only hired those with high scores. Managers began complaining that employees didn't work well together. Customers weren't happy with the service they received."

Statement 3

"We evaluated the traits that our most successful employees shared. These skills included conflict management, the ability to handle change, empathy, integrity, and the ability to read others' emotions and react appropriately."

Statement 4

"Now, we look for employees who are 'people smart.' They know how to resolve conflicts and motivate others.

Our star employees have a range of IQs, but share one common trait--they're high in emotional intelligence."

Brenda is hiring a new manager for the technical service department, which is the main center for customer contact. This person will be responsible for 15 representatives who help customers resolve computer problems. If the technical service department doesn't run smoothly, the company's reputation will suffer.

The first candidate Brenda evaluates is Ken, a highly skilled technical service representative. The second is Amber, who has experience managing customer service departments.

See each candidate to reveal Brenda's assessment.

Ken

"Ken is a great representative, but management is about working with others. Ken prefers to work on his own, so I don't think he's a good fit."

Amber

"Amber is skilled at motivating people, even in extremely challenging situations. Amber has demonstrated leadership skills. She's the best choice."

Brenda didn't focus on hiring the "smartest" job candidate. Instead, she looked for the employee who demonstrated the skills needed for the job. It's easy to be misled into thinking that the most intelligent job candidate will be the best fit.

Emotional intelligence skills are often more important to a good job fit than IQ or academic achievement. Look for the best all-around candidate.

Question

Which are common misconceptions about intelligence?

Options:

1. Career success can be predicted based on IQ.
2. The most successful companies hire employees with the highest IQs.
3. The best job candidates have the highest IQs.
4. IQ alone does not predict career success.
5. Emotional intelligence can be more important in the workplace than academic intelligence.

Answer:

Actually, misconceptions about intelligence include the idea that career success can be predicted by IQ, that successful companies hire the "smartest" employees, and that the best job candidates are the smartest job candidates.

Option 1: This answer is correct. That career success can be predicted based on IQ is a common misconception. While a certain IQ may be needed to enter a field like engineering, academic intelligence alone does not equal workplace achievement.

Option 2: Correct. A common misconception is successful companies hire employees with the highest IQs. Companies need people who have a wide range of skills that cannot be measured by test scores or grades.

Option 3: Correct. A common misconception is the best job candidates have the highest IQs. Emotional intelligence skills are often more important to a good job fit than IQ. Companies want the best all-around candidates.

Option 4: This answer is incorrect. That IQ alone does not predict career success is not a misconception because intelligence alone does not equal workplace achievement.

Option 5: Incorrect. That emotional intelligence can be more important than academic intelligence in the workplace is not a misconception because companies look for a wider range of skills than simply academic intelligence.

There are many common misperceptions about intelligence. Remember, IQ is not the most important factor in workplace effectiveness. Many other qualities, such as emotional effectiveness, are important for success as well.

What does it mean to be intelligent? Is it IQ? Common sense? The ability to get along with others?

Intelligence at work is made up of three factors. The presence or lack of any of these factors affects a person's "intelligence." The most successful workers are strong in the following areas:
- IQ (intelligence quotient),
- expertise,
- emotional intelligence.

Question
How important is IQ to job success?
Options:
1. none
2. 25 percent
3. 50 percent
4. 75 percent
5. 100 percent

Answer:
Studies indicate that IQ accounts for only 4 percent to 25 percent of on-the-job success. That means that at least 75 percent of job success is determined by factors other than IQ.

IQ is a threshold competency. It's necessary to have a certain IQ to work in many professions. But once you meet the threshold requirement of that field, IQ then accounts for only 4 percent to 25 percent of career success.

An IQ of at least 120 might be the threshold to become a doctor. However, a doctor with an IQ of 140 isn't necessarily more successful than another doctor with an IQ of 130.

Expertise includes technical knowledge, training, and experience. It's the background people receive when they work at a job.

See each statement for more information about expertise.

Expertise is more important than IQ

In some ways, expertise is more important than IQ. After all, you can be a genius, but without specific training, you aren't qualified to be a doctor.

Expertise is a threshold competency

Expertise is a threshold competency. You need expertise to enter a field, but your technical knowledge alone won't get you to the top.

Since IQ and expertise alone can't account for all intelligence, what's the missing factor?

It's emotional intelligence--the ability to handle emotions appropriately and work well with others. See each aspect for more information about emotional intelligence.

Synergy

Emotional intelligence works with IQ and expertise--a top performer has all of these qualities. Workplace ability begins with intellect. Education and experience build the next layer. Emotional intelligence is the final component.

When it matters most

The more complex and high-level the job, the more important emotional intelligence becomes. A lack of emotional intelligence can detract from IQ and expertise, and make it difficult to work with or to manage teams.

When smart is stupid

When emotions rage out of control, smart people can act stupid. They may yell, say hurtful things, lower morale, even drive away customers. Because a lack of control can be damaging, emotional intelligence is especially important in the workplace.

Question

Practice what you've learned. Match IQ, expertise, and emotional intelligence with one or more appropriate contributions to workplace ability.

Options:

A. expertise
B. IQ
C. emotional intelligence

Targets:

1. especially important in complex jobs
2. accounts for 4 percent to 25 percent of job success
3. accounts for slightly more job success than IQ
4. knowledge gained by working in a field

Answer:

Actually, IQ accounts for 4 percent to 25 percent of job success; expertise accounts for slightly more and is gained on the job. Emotional intelligence is especially important in complex jobs.

Emotional intelligence is especially important in complex jobs because a lack of emotional intelligence can detract from IQ and expertise, and make it difficult to work with or to manage teams.

IQ accounts for 4 percent to 25 percent of job success. It is necessary to have a certain IQ to work in many professions, but once you reach the threshold, expertise and emotional intelligence account for the rest.

Expertise accounts for slightly more job success than IQ. It is a threshold competency needed to enter a field, but your technical knowledge alone will not get you to the top.

Expertise is knowledge gained by working in a field and includes technical knowledge, training, and experience. The background experience people receive when they work at a job is expertise.

Intelligence in the workplace is a combination of three domains: IQ, expertise, and emotional intelligence. IQ and expertise are threshold competencies; they're sometimes required to enter a field. However, once these requirements are met, emotional intelligence accounts for the majority of on-the-job success.

Phil has been one of the top-performing sales people at his company for the past five years. His manager, Darlene, describes him as a great people person. He keeps customers satisfied. When problems occur, he's a great mediator between the home office and the customer. He doesn't get frazzled in high-pressure situations.

What makes Phil different from other sales people?

Phil is emotionally "competent," which helps him be a top performer. Successful employees are able to manage a wide range of emotions, and deal with other people effectively. Emotional intelligence abilities fall into two main categories:

- personal abilities, which include self-awareness, self-management, and goal orientation,

- social abilities, which include empathy and social skills.

The first set of abilities is "personal" abilities. These skills refer to how you manage yourself. These competencies include self-awareness, self-management, and goal orientation.

See each personal ability for its definition.

self-awareness

Self-awareness means being aware of emotions, strengths and limits, and capabilities. It means having a strong understanding of yourself and what you do well, and your areas of weakness.

self-management

Self-management means controlling emotions and impulses. It means having integrity. It also includes being flexible, responsible, and innovative. Instead of holding others responsible for your success, you take action yourself.

goal orientation

Goal orientation is the emotional ability that helps you reach a goal. It includes the desire to achieve, your level of commitment, your initiative, and a positive attitude.

Darlene is discussing Phil's personal competencies with John, another manager. John's interested in the impact of these competencies on performance.

John: How does Phil's self-awareness make a difference at work?

Darlene: He knows that his mood affects his customer's mood. If he is tense, his customers will pick up on this. He projects a positive attitude, which is contagious.

John: How about his awareness of his limitations? How does that make a difference?

Darlene: He knows that he needs to spend extra time learning about technical issues since they're not his strong point.

John: It seems like self-management would be especially important in sales. Can you give me an example?

Darlene: Phil never flies off the handle, even in high-pressure situations. He takes a proactive approach to solving problems instead of blaming others.

John: How does Phil's motivation make him a great performer?

Darlene: Phil sets high goals for himself and dedicates his time to reaching those goals.

The second set of abilities is "social" abilities. These skills determine how well you deal with others. See each social ability and how to use it at work for more information.

Empathy

Empathy means being aware of other people's feelings, needs, and concerns. It includes taking an interest in others' concerns and helping them develop their abilities.

Social skills

People with strong social skills are able to solicit effective responses from others. They are able to communicate well with others, have strong conflict management skills, and exhibit leadership skills.

Empathy at work

Empathy is especially important with customers, because anticipating and meeting their needs is critical to success in the workplace. Customers want suppliers to take an active interest in their concerns.

Social skills at work

Social skills are important for interacting with customers and co-workers. Those with strong social skills are able to work well in team environments. They are also able to lead effectively since they can influence others in positive directions.

Question

Identify the emotional intelligence attributes in top performers.

Options:

1. empathy
2. self-denial
3. independence
4. self-regulation
5. motivation

Answer:

Actually, empathy, self-regulation, and motivation are emotional intelligence attributes in top performers.

Option 1: This answer is correct. Empathy is an attribute of top performers because anticipating and meeting needs is critical to success in the workplace.

Option 2: This answer is incorrect. Self-denial is not an attribute of top performers. They tend not to deny themselves of things, but they do exhibit self-control.

Option 3: This answer is incorrect. While top performers may be independent when the situation calls for it, independence is not one of the emotional intelligence attributes found in top performers.

Option 4: This answer is correct. Self-regulation is an attribute of top performers and it is exemplified by controlling emotions and impulses. It means having integrity, being flexible, responsible, and innovative.

Option 5: This answer is correct. Top performers are motivated, they set high goals for themselves and dedicate their time to reaching those goals.

Top performers in the workplace have a wide range of competencies. In addition to their intelligence and training, these workers have emotional intelligence abilities. Remember that these abilities fall into two groups:
- personal abilities, which include self-awareness, self-regulation, and motivation,
- social abilities, which include empathy and social skills.
-

SELF-ASSESSMENT AT WORK

Self-assessment at Work

Have you ever heard the saying, "knowledge is power"? If that is true, then knowledge about yourself is especially important. If you don't understand yourself, how can you understand anything else?

Your knowledge about yourself can significantly affect your work life. An accurate self-assessment will help you improve your strengths and minimize your weaknesses. In this lesson, you'll explore:

- the importance of gut feelings,
- the benefits of an accurate self-assessment,
- how confidence impacts your career.

Question

What is the value of becoming more self-aware?

Options:

1. Self-awareness will improve people's abilities in their areas of expertise.

2. Self-awareness will help improve one's weaknesses.

3. Self-awareness is critical to self-improvement.

4. Self-awareness positively affects career success.

Answer:

Actually, self-awareness will positively affect your career. You'll understand your strengths and weaknesses, and will have enough information to positively improve yourself.

Option 1: This answer is incorrect. Self-awareness will not improve expertise, because enhanced expertise comes through education or experience in a given subject area.

Option 2: This answer is correct. Self-awareness and confidence will help improve weaknesses because you will recognize your weak areas, seek improvement through training and education, and seek help for tasks in your areas of weakness.

Option 3: This answer is correct. Self-awareness and assessment are critical to self-improvement because you will know yourself and understand your weak areas.

Option 4: This answer is correct. Self-awareness positively affects career success because you will know your strengths and use them to your advantage as well as understand areas you need to improve upon.

During this lesson, you'll begin to understand the source and importance of gut feelings and the powerful role that intuition plays in decision making. You'll also gain insight into the blind spots that make self-evaluation difficult.

You'll explore the importance of self-confidence in your career and how low confidence can derail your professional life.

The proposal for the new business sounded great. The financial statements were strong, the mission was clear, and the partners were experienced. Lots of people invested with the approval of their financial advisers. A year later, the business was bankrupt. Thousands of people lost money. Gloria was one of the people who held on to her money instead of investing. Did Gloria know something that no one else did? "It was just instinct," Gloria said. "The proposal just didn't sit right with me."

Is there really such a thing as instinct? Does instinct make a difference?

Question

How often do you use instincts to make decisions?

Options:

1. never
2. sometimes
3. half the time
4. most of the time
5. always

Answer:

Instincts can be a valuable part of the decision-making process. Most experts recommend that you use both gut feelings and facts when making choices.

Instincts can be an important part of the decision-making process. Many high-ranking executives report that their gut-level reactions factor into critical decisions, such as mergers, financial moves, and other high-impact situations.

In this lesson, you'll explore the source of instincts and how intuitive feelings change with age, and you'll answer the question, "How much of my gut reaction should I rely on?"

Where do instincts come from? Are they part of our imagination? Psychic powers? Or are they part of the brain's natural function?

Instincts are a part of the brain's learning system.

See each question to learn more about how instincts work.

Where do instincts come from?

Every experience you have evokes an emotion--fear, happiness, or contentment. These emotions are stored in a part of the brain called the amygdala. This provides you with an "emotional blueprint" of every experience you've had.

Instincts or gut feelings may come from an essential early warning system for danger that is still present today in feelings such as anxiety or apprehension. Instinct is like primitive radar--telling you that something is "off."

What does the amygdala do?

The amygdala uses this information to help you make decisions like, "The fish sounds better than the pasta." It's through this part of the brain that you have gut reactions to each decision you're faced with.

Instincts come from remembered emotional patterns. Life experiences add up, so it's logical that older people have more gut feelings than younger people.

Older people also have stronger instincts than younger people. They've also learned to trust their inner radar.

What should you do when something just doesn't feel right? Should you ignore the feeling or listen to it? There are many ways to deal with gut feelings, but the best approach is to balance feelings with facts.

- Pay attention to your intuition.
- Instincts shouldn't outweigh the facts, but you should consider them with the facts.
- These gut feelings often tell you how each choice will fit in with your big picture, values, and

preferences. If a choice feels "off," it may be wrong.

Question

Which statements about the characteristics of instincts are true?

Options:

1. Young people usually have stronger instincts than older people.

2. Instincts come from stored emotional reactions to other life events.

3. Instincts should be ignored since they are only emotional reactions.

4. Instincts become stronger with more life experience.

Answer:

Actually, instincts come from emotional reactions to life events that are stored in a part of the brain called the amygdala. Instincts become stronger with life experience, since more reactions can be stored.

Option 1: This answer is incorrect. Because instincts come from remembered emotional patterns and life experiences that add up, it is logical that older people have stronger instincts than younger people.

Option 2: Correct. Instincts come from stored emotional reactions to other life events. These emotions are stored in a part of the brain called the amygdala, which provides an "emotional blueprint" of every experience you have had.

Option 3: Incorrect. Some instinctual reactions seem to be emotionally based, but they should not be ignored. You should consider them with the facts because they tell you how each choice will fit in with your big picture, values, and preferences.

Option 4: This answer is correct. Instincts become stronger as we age because they come from remembered emotional patterns. Life experiences add up, which means older people have more gut feelings than younger people.

Instincts are thought to be a warning system, like radar. They developed in the brain through evolution, like many other thought processes. The following points are important in understanding instincts.

- Instincts come from a part of the brain called the amygdala.
- Instincts grow over time, so gut feelings tend to get stronger with age.
- Consider instincts and facts when making decisions.

Bill managed a team of service technicians. His motto was, "I'm a hands-off manager." He told his team members that he wanted to empower them and wouldn't interfere in their day-to-day activities.

But when a problem popped up, Bill immediately started micromanaging. "Bill thinks he's hands-off, but he's really a control freak," said one of the technicians. "I don't want to work for him anymore."

Bill isn't accurately judging himself. He thinks he's a liberal manager, but his employees see him as a controlling micromanager. Bill has blind spots, which are a common barrier to accurate self-assessment. In this topic, you'll learn:

- why it's important to have an accurate self-assessment,
- how blind spots interfere with self-evaluation,
- examples of typical blind spots.

A blind spot is a barrier to accurate self-assessment. It's something you don't see about yourself. Bill thinks he's a hands-off manager, but his style is very controlling. Blind spots like Bill's can derail your career. If you don't see negative behavior, you can't change it. If Bill doesn't change his management style, he could lose employees who are good at their jobs.

He could also be passed up for a promotion or even lose his job because he doesn't see himself clearly. Bill's boss, Anna, is going to talk to him about his management style.

Anna, Bill's manager, is attempting to give Bill feedback about his performance. Follow his reaction to her feedback.

Anna: Bill, could you tell me a little bit about how you see your relationship with your employees? I'd like to get your perspective.

Bill: I think I have a great relationship with my staff members. I'm pretty hands-off--they're free to make their own decisions. I think they're pretty happy.

Anna: I noticed the last time we had a breakdown, you took the reins. The staff didn't seem to have much input.

Bill: Well, in an emergency situation, it's important for a manager to step in. I can't risk a mistake by someone else.

Anna: But aren't your staff members trained for just this kind of emergency? It seems that you could empower them by letting them take the lead.

Bill: I'm ultimately responsible. I don't see it as an empowerment issue--I have to make the decisions because I'm the manager.

Bill is in denial. It's too hard for him to admit that he may be making mistakes, so he's ignoring the negative information. He has made excuses, but the problem still exists. Other denial techniques include minimizing facts and rationalizing.

Bill's denial strategy is helping him ignore the facts, so he doesn't have to change. Admitting the problem would be the first step toward change.

There are eight common blind spots that interfere with accurate self-assessment. Four are given here; the remaining four are listed on the following page.

See each blind spot type for an example.

Excessive ambition

"Fred feels like he has to be right, no matter what the cost. He doesn't cooperate--he competes, even with people on his own team. Other people think he's arrogant and that he brags too much about his accomplishments."

Unreasonable goals

"It's almost impossible for Kate's team to meet the deadlines she sets. She doesn't understand how much time and effort it takes to complete tasks, so she's not sympathetic when team members struggle."

Workaholism

"Matt is a workaholic. His job takes precedence over everything else in his life. He's compromised his family to work long and, often, unnecessary hours. He's almost burnt out--so when there's an emergency, he can't cope effectively."

Pushing others

"Jodie pushes her team members too hard--they're on the verge of a breakdown. She's a micromanager; she takes over and doesn't let her staff make even small decisions. Staff members describe her as cold blooded."

The remaining four common blind spots are described here.

Read about each employee to learn how managers describe employees with blind spots.

Hunger for power

"Tracey is hungry for power. She wants authority to further her own self-interests. She always has her agenda and isn't concerned about anyone else's needs. She's always out for herself."

Glory seeking

"Bart is a glory seeker. He takes credit for other people's work, but is quick to shift the blame for mistakes. He also doesn't follow through on projects. After he's been praised, he's out looking for the next parade, instead of finishing tasks."

Focused on appearance

"Ralph is very concerned about appearances and wants to make sure he looks good. He cares more about how expensive his suit is than how his employees are doing. He doesn't worry as much about the product as he does about his image."

Perfectionism

"Denise is a perfectionist. She is focused on small details, even when the big picture is more important. She doesn't take feedback well and often becomes angry. She doesn't admit to mistakes, even when she's clearly at fault."

Question

What are the common blind spots that hinder accurate self-assessment?

Options:
1. excessive ambition
2. work-life balance
3. unreasonable goals
4. hunger for power
5. goal orientation

Answer:

Actually, excessive ambition, unreasonable goals, and hunger for power are common blind spots. These barriers can prevent you from seeing yourself clearly.

Option 1: This answer is correct. Excessive ambition is a common blind spot. Individuals with this blind spot usually have to be right no matter what the cost and are overly competitive even with members of their own team.

Option 2: This answer is incorrect. Work-life balance is not a blind spot because you are not placing excessive importance on one part of your life, your job.

Option 3: This answer is correct. Unreasonable goals hinder accurate self-assessment because these types of goals set yourself or others up for failure. Deadlines and expectations are impossible to meet.

Option 4: This answer is correct. A common blind spot is the hunger for power. People with this trait aren't concerned about anyone else's needs. They are always out for themselves.

Option 5: This answer is incorrect. Goal orientation will not hinder accurate self-assessment because it focuses on the big picture.

An accurate self-assessment helps you understand yourself. Blind spots can interfere with your ability to see yourself clearly. It's easy to slip into denial and filter out negative information.

By understanding blind spots and seeking feedback from others, you can increase your self-awareness.

Why is confidence important? Because it predicts career success. Those with confidence tend to do well in the workplace, while those without it usually fall behind.

Why is confidence such an important factor in career success? It helps leaders stand out. Confidence becomes more important as you progress in your career. In this topic, you'll explore:

- the drawbacks of too little confidence,
- the effect of confidence on workplace success,
- the importance of courage.

What contribution does confidence make in the workplace? Your confidence level affects many aspects of your work life.

See each factor for more information on how confidence can affect your career:

leadership

Leaders need confidence to get into management and supervisory positions. If you don't have confidence, you won't seek out positions of responsibility. You won't have enough faith in your abilities to assume leadership.

decision making

If you have confidence in yourself, you'll believe that your opinions have merit. You'll be able to weigh options and have faith that you're choosing the best course of action. Without confidence, you'll avoid making decisions out of fear of making mistakes.

facing opposition

You may have to make decisions or take actions that aren't supported by everyone. If you have enough confidence, you'll be able to handle opposition. People without confidence won't stand up to others--they'll cave at the first sign of disagreement or disapproval.

inspiring confidence in others

If you have faith in yourself, it's easy to inspire confidence in others. Others can sense your faith in yourself through what you say. If you say things like, "I'm not sure I can do this," people will assume you can't.

ambition

If you have confidence, you'll have more ambition. You'll be motivated to achieve because you believe in yourself. Without confidence, you'll avoid challenges because you won't have the ability to bounce back from mistakes.

seeking opportunities

If you have confidence, it's easier to approach others about opportunities such as jobs, exciting projects, and promotions. If you have little confidence, you'll be too afraid of rejection to seek out opportunities--and you'll miss out.

Diane worked in the software development division of a large company. Her boss decided to implement a software tracking device, which Diane knew would corrupt much of the department's data. The cost would have been nearly $1 million. She tried repeatedly to talk to her boss, but despite numerous protests by Diane and other staff members, he went ahead with his plan. Since her boss wouldn't listen, Diane decided to go over his head. The problem was immediately resolved.

When asked about her decision, Diane said, "I couldn't risk such a large cost to the company to protect someone's ego. I knew it was risky to go over my boss's head, but I knew the biggest risk was letting his plan move forward."

Did Diane take the right risk? She saved the company a lot of money by taking the right step at the right time. Diane didn't act from selfish motives--she had the interests of everyone in mind.
- Courage matters when the risks of not speaking out are greater than the risks of staying quiet.
- Courage should be based on an understanding of the facts and of your ability to judge the facts.
- Courage should be motivated by what's in everyone's best interests.

Question
Identify how confidence affects career success.

Options:
1. Confidence is needed for making tough decisions.
2. Confidence lowers ambition.
3. Confidence is an accurate predictor of career success.
4. Confidence helps in overcoming failures.
5. Confidence increases indecisiveness.

Answer:
Actually, confidence is important in career success. Those with confidence are more likely to be successful. They'll be able to make tough decisions and overcome failures.

Option 1: This answer is correct. Confidence is needed for making tough decisions because you'll be able to weigh options and have faith that you're choosing the best course of action.

Option 2: This answer in incorrect. Confidence and ambition go hand-in-hand, so one would not lessen the other.

Option 3: Correct. Confidence is an accurate predictor of career success. If you have confidence, it's easier to approach others about jobs opportunities, exciting projects, and promotions. You'll be motivated to achieve because you believe in yourself.

Option 4: This answer is correct. Confidence helps you to overcome failures because without confidence, you'll avoid challenges since you won't have the ability to bounce back from mistakes.

Option 5: This choice is incorrect. Confidence actually decreases indecisiveness. Without confidence, you would avoid making decisions out of fear of making mistakes.

Confidence is an important factor in career success. Your self-assurance is your ability to pursue opportunities, make decisions, and face opposition. Confidence is also necessary in order to act with courage in particular situations.

A lack of confidence can negatively affect your ability to move forward in your career. Self-assurance is a key factor in workplace success.

SELF-MANAGEMENT AND CONTROL

Self-management and Control

Have you ever seen someone rage out of control, have a temper tantrum, yell and scream? Does this behavior solve problems, or does it make things worse?

Everyone has emotions--ranging from contentment to anger. Some people are able to control their emotions, while others damage relationships and lose productivity. In this lesson, you'll explore:

- the skills needed to keep emotions and impulses under control,
- the importance of integrity to good working relationships,
- the tools you need to "change with change.

Question

What are the benefits of regulating and controlling your emotions?

Options:

1. You can improve your relationship with management.

2. You will improve your chances for leadership roles.

3. You can avoid unproductive conflict.

4. You will become better at time management.

Answer:

Actually, by controlling your emotions, you'll build better relationships and work through problems productively. You'll also be able to improve your chances for leadership roles.

Option 1: This answer is correct. Keeping emotions in check can improve your relationship with management because you will be a more reliable employee.

Option 2: This answer is correct. Regulating and controlling your emotions will improve your chances for leadership roles because you will be viewed as a reliable and responsible individual.

Option 3: This choice is correct. Regulating and controlling your emotions means you can avoid unproductive conflict because you will avoid situations that may cause issues and be prepared to handle individuals in a productive manner.

Option 4: This answer is incorrect. Regulating and controlling your emotions will not necessarily make you a better time manager, but it will enable you to avoid situations that you know will cause conflict and result in a poor use of your time.

Work life is filled with ups and downs. It's normal to experience a wide range of emotion toward business turmoil. Your management of your emotions and impulses is what sets you apart from your co-workers.

In this lesson, you'll learn about the skills that help you adapt to the changing business environment: responsibility, building trust, innovation, and adaptability.

Emotional Intelligence at Work

Jeanine is a front-line customer service representative. One day, a customer came to her counter and began yelling because of a costly mistake on his bill.

The other representatives watched in amazement as Jeanine handled the situation. "I can imagine how frustrated you feel," she said calmly. "I'd be upset too." The customer's anger began to dissolve and Jeanine was able to solve his problem without his becoming upset again.

How does Jeanine do it? She has a lot of self-control and she's able to manage her emotions. Instead of letting feelings dictate how she behaves, she controls her moods. In this topic, you'll learn:

- what self-control means,
- how emotional-intelligence skills help you control emotions.

Question

Think of the people you know who manage to stay calm under most circumstances, then decide whether the following statement is true or false.

Calm, relaxed people have fewer emotions than those who are easily upset.

Options:

1. true
2. false

Answer:

Actually, people who appear calm still have emotions. They use and control their emotions differently than people who often appear visibly upset.

Option 1: This statement is not true. If relaxed people had fewer emotions than those who are easily upset, they would not have the range that allows them to appear calm in tense situations.

Option 2: This statement is false. It's not that relaxed people have fewer emotions, but rather they know how to handle them in stressful situations.

People with emotional self-restraint don't tend to come unglued in stressful situations. Like Jeanine, they can manage someone else's tantrum without becoming angry. Other characteristics of self-control include the following:

- **mood management:** Some people recognize and control their moods. They change behaviors that cause bad moods.
- **self-understanding:** Some people are very aware of their strengths and weaknesses and seek help when appropriate.
- **calmness under fire:** Remaining calm defuses an attacker's emotions.
- **clarity about feelings:** People who understand their feelings can manage them.

Just because someone holds in emotions doesn't mean he is coping effectively. Some people don't react visibly, but their negative emotions come out in other ways. High blood pressure, headaches, backaches, and other kinds of health problems can be caused by holding negative feelings in. It's important to understand and release stress. Coping techniques vary depending on your preferences. Think about what makes you feel better.

Remember, it's not wrong to have bad feelings. It's what you do with those feelings that matters. Don't use negative emotions to create more unpleasant situations. When you face stress, find a way to cope and turn the situation into a positive one.

Emotional Intelligence at Work

There are four important skills that help you keep your emotions in check. The first two are managing your moods and understanding yourself. These mean not letting moods rule your behavior, and knowing your strengths and weaknesses well enough to manage stress. The second two skills are remaining calm under fire and understanding your feelings. If you can remain neutral under attack, you can deflect many problems. If you understand your feelings, you can seek to improve relationships.

See each person to learn how these emotional self-control skills can work.

Diego

"I know I get grouchy in the afternoons. Instead of wasting my time being angry, I schedule a task I enjoy for the afternoon. I really like meeting with team members, so I try to schedule a meeting with someone upbeat."

Mabel

"One of my co-workers makes me very tense, so I rehearse before I have to talk to her. Because I know she makes me tense, it's important for me to think about what I want from our conversation. If I plan ahead, I won't get emotional."

Jason

"I know customers can get pretty upset. I also know I have to remain calm, or the situation will just get worse. I count to ten before I respond to anything an angry customer says. That way I have to think before I speak."

Noelle

"I know that I get tense when I have to crunch numbers. I have someone else check my work so I don't worry and end up panicking. They help me understand where I make mistakes, so over time, I'm getting better."

Question

Identify the skills that enable individuals to keep emotions and impulses in check.

Options:

1. thinking clearly under pressure
2. understanding your own feelings
3. managing time
4. ignoring emotional stress

Answer:

Actually, people who keep impulses and emotions regulated are able to remain composed and positive even under tense circumstances. They are able to manage their life to avoid stressful situations.

Option 1: This choice is correct. Thinking clearly under pressure is a skill that keeps emotions and impulses in check because remaining calm will diffuse difficult situations.

Option 2: This is a correct answer. Understanding your own feelings can keep emotions and impulses in check because you don't let your moods rule your behavior.

Option 3: This answer is correct. Managing your time helps keep emotions and impulses in check because you will not waste your time being angry or upset if you are aware of what triggers your emotional reactions and avoid those situations.

Option 4: This answer is incorrect. Ignoring emotional stress is not a skill that will keep emotions in check because the emotional stress may surface in other ways like high blood pressure, headaches, backaches, and other kinds of health problems.

Remember, having strong self-control doesn't mean avoiding emotions. It means dealing with emotions effectively. You can get control over your feelings by gaining understanding.

It's also important to understand your feelings and abilities so you can plan positive actions.

"I knew I had to fire Ted the minute I saw his expense report," reported Ellen, a sales manager. "We'd been to dinner together almost every night, so I knew what his bills were. His reports were only off by a few dollars, but if he was willing to lie about a small amount of money, what else would he lie about? How can I trust someone like that with my customers?"

Integrity is an important, but often overlooked, factor in career success. People with integrity tend to stand out favorably from their peers. In this topic, you'll explore:
- the importance of honesty,
- the value of impulse control,
- the effect of accountability.

Question

Which examples of dishonesty are common in the workplace?

Options:

1. taking credit for someone else's work
2. forgery
3. giving false information to a supervisor
4. lying to a customer
5. stealing office supplies

Answer:

Actually, these are all common examples of workplace dishonesty. While they vary in severity, all of these types of dishonesty negatively affect the company in some way.

Option 1: This is a correct choice. An example of dishonesty in the workplace is taking credit for someone else's work. This can be damaging to the company as a whole and the individuals involved.

Option 2: This answer is correct. Forgery is an example of dishonesty in the workplace, and depending on the specifics can be very damaging to the organization.

Option 3: This answer is correct. Giving false information to a supervisor is dishonest and could be damaging to the company and the individual's career.

Option 4: This answer is correct. An example of dishonesty is lying to a customer. Ultimately, this could damage the company because they would lose a lot of money and business because of this behavior.

Option 5: This answer is correct. Stealing office supplies is an example of dishonesty in the workplace because it could cost the company a lot of money.

Employers notice and value honesty in employees. Integrity is good for business. Jeff is a warehouse supervisor.

See each of his comments about workers and integrity to learn more.

Honesty is important

"My workers could steal supplies and lie to customers. Ultimately, we could lose a lot of money and business because of this behavior. I can't afford to hire people I don't trust. The cost could be high."

Ethical behavior

"I know some people call in sick when they just want to enjoy a day off. But if I happen to find out, I'm less tempted to trust those people because they've shown a history of lying."

Being frank

"When people are honest with me, I know that I can trust them. If an employee admits a mistake or tells me about a problem, I know she'll be honest with me about other problems. I can trust that person to tell me the truth."

Building trust

"It takes time to trust someone. If an employee follows through on commitments, no matter how small the promise, I know I can trust that person. However, I don't trust people who don't follow through."

What about people who don't have a lot of integrity? Studies show they have low self-restraint. They aren't able to delay gratification, even when they can see a reward further down the road.

People with impulse control think about the consequences before they act. This kind of maturity pays off in the long run.

A person with low impulse control thinks: "I know I have an important meeting today, but it's the first day of spring. I'm calling in sick." This behavior has a negative effect on careers over time.

Reliability is an important key to success in any work environment. See each employee to learn how reliability can play out at work.

Pam

Pam comes to work every day at 8 a.m. She rarely calls in sick. Her assignments are orderly and completed on time.

Aaron

Aaron does great work, but his schedule is erratic. His boss doesn't know when or where to find him. His assignments are often late or incomplete.

Pam is more likely to be promoted than Aaron. Supervisors tend to rate reliable people better on reviews than less-dependable workers. People like Pam are the backbone of companies. They follow the rules, keep up to date on information, and meet deadlines. These are valuable qualities at every level within an organization.

Question

What are the characteristics of integrity?

Options:

1. telling an untruth in order to protect someone from embarrassment

2. holding yourself accountable for meeting goals

3. concealing information in order to protect a co-worker's feelings

4. telling the truth, even when it's not easy

5. delaying gratification

Answer:

Actually, people with integrity act ethically. They act honestly and expect appropriate behavior from others. They can sacrifice immediate gratification when appropriate.

Option 1: This answer is incorrect. Telling an untruth even if it is motivated by friendship or loyalty is unethical and shows a lack of integrity.

Option 2: This answer is correct. Holding yourself accountable for meeting goals shows integrity because it shows a level of reliability which is very important in the workplace.

Option 3: This answer is incorrect. Concealing information in order to protect a co-worker's feelings is not a characteristic of integrity because even though the action is motivated out of kindness, it is still unethical.

Option 4: This answer is correct. Telling the truth, even when it's not easy is a characteristic of integrity because it means you will be honest about other problems that may surface.

Option 5: This answer is correct. Delaying gratification is a characteristic of integrity because thinking about the consequences before you act pays off in the long run.

It's easy to forget how qualities such as reliability, impulse control, and honesty can be so important in work life. Remember, these behaviors strongly contribute to other people's impressions of you.

"It is not the strongest of the species that survive, nor the most intelligent, but the one most responsive to change." --Charles Darwin

Successful people in today's business environment are able to flexibly respond to change. Your career and mental health can suffer if you don't change along with your environment. In this topic, you'll learn:

- how innovation can help you be effective,
- why adaptability is an important skill.

Have you ever heard the expression "innovate or die"? This saying demonstrates the importance of coming up with new ideas. It isn't easy to be creative--it often means going against tradition. However, people who refuse to be innovative have a difficult time solving problems because they're opposed to new ideas. They often miss the big picture because they focus on the small details. Innovators are the people who help foster change.

See each aspect to learn more about innovators.

Information

Innovators seek out information from lots of sources-- they talk to customers, other workers, and management. They use this information to figure out the needs that are developing and how these needs can be met.

"Crazy" ideas

Innovators aren't bound by convention. They consider ideas that might seem crazy or impossible. Think about how bizarre the Wright brothers' flying machine must have sounded. Today, flying is a major industry.

Generating Ideas

Innovators come up with a lot of ideas. Some may work; others won't be successful. However, the practice of generating ideas is important. If an innovator doesn't brainstorm, no new products and services can be created.

Passion

Innovators love new ideas. This is how they create unusual solutions to problems. This "originality" is an important business edge. The crazy ideas of today are the lucrative products of tomorrow.

It's important to constantly scan and take in new information about the environment. People who ignore feedback from customers and employees may miss out on critical information about needs and problems.

In 1943, computers weren't a major industry, but 40 years later, the computer boom began. If IBM had kept the 1943 attitude, the company would have missed out on a major opportunity.

What should you do when your environment changes? According to the theories of evolution, you either adapt to fit the changes or you become obsolete. In the business world, this means falling behind competitors and losing customers.

Your ability to "change with change" is valuable. Adapters, people who respond well to change, are becoming more and more important to the companies they work for:

- Adapters can handle multiple tasks. They can easily change priorities.
- Adapters can change their responses and tactics to fit new circumstances. They don't panic in new situations.
- Adapters are flexible enough to take in new information. They don't protect themselves from painful information such as, "You're doing this the wrong way."
- Adapters are emotionally strong. They are comfortable with ambiguity.

Question

What are the characteristics of innovation and adaptability? Match each attribute with one or more corresponding descriptions.

Options:

A. innovation
B. adaptability

Targets:

1. creates unusual solutions to problems
2. generates new ways of accomplishing goals

3. helps multitasks run more smoothly

4. meets multiple demands

Answer:

Actually, adaptability is the ability to face the unexpected. Innovation is taking pleasure in originality.

Innovation creates unusual solutions to problems because innovators have a passion for new ideas.

Innovation generates new ways of accomplishing goals. Because innovators aren't bound by convention, they consider ideas that might seem crazy or impossible to others.

Adaptability helps multitasks run more smoothly because the person adapting can easily change priorities.

Adaptability means the person adapting is flexible enough to meet the multiple demands of the job.

What skills will most help you in your career? Your ability to change and adapt to your environment will set you apart. As customer needs develop, you'll have to find new ideas and products.

Remember, customers and employees are important sources of information about change. If you keep up to date, you'll be able to respond effectively.

PROVIDING SELF-MOTIVATION

Providing Self-motivation

No matter what job you find yourself in, you'll always be dealing with the same coach--a coach who will help you fail or succeed. That coach is you.

You ultimately have the most power over your own success. By learning to motivate yourself, you'll be able to control your own career destiny. In this lesson, you'll explore three important components.
- striving for excellence,
- commitment and loyalty,
- surviving change.

Question

Melanie wants career advice. Help her by explaining the value of being able to motivate oneself.

Options:

1. She'll ensure that her career will be fulfilling.
2. She'll help herself be successful.
3. She'll be better able to deal with change.
4. She'll be promoted into a management position.
5. She'll be able to recover from setbacks.

Answer:

Actually, by motivating yourself, you'll be able to cope in a wide variety of situations. You'll recover from setbacks and you will help yourself meet ambitious goals.

Option 1: This answer is incorrect. Being self-motivated will not ensure Melanie that her career will be fulfilling, unless she has chosen something she truly believes in.

Option 2: This answer is correct. Being able to motivate herself will help Melanie be successful because she will strive to do better and seek out constructive criticism.

Option 3: This answer is correct. Being able to motivate herself means Melanie will view change optimistically. Optimists tend to shed a positive light on events. They find a positive response, even in trying situations.

Option 4: This answer is incorrect. Being self-motivated will not ensure that Melanie is promoted into management, but it will give her an advantage over someone who is not.

Option 5: This answer is correct. Being able to motivate herself means Melanie will be able to recover from setbacks. She will see setbacks as a challenge and will not take them personally.

You can have the most impact on your own motivation. By increasing your skills in this area, you'll be able to effectively meet goals and move ahead in your career. You'll explore how striving for excellence, commitment, and surviving change work together to lead to success.

Why do some people leap ahead in their careers? Does a desire to succeed matter? Do successful people do something different?

Studies show that successful people share similar behavior. In this topic, you'll explore some of these actions and attitudes, including:
- setting challenging goals,
- taking calculated risks,
- constantly gathering information,
- actively seeking feedback.

Tina and Sam, two computer programmers, are both setting their goals for the next performance quarter. Sam knows that he'll get a decent performance review if he finishes his program in six months and sets his goals accordingly. Tina knows it will be acceptable if she finishes her program in six months; however, she knows a quicker timeline will help the company be more profitable. She aims to exceed expectations and finishes her program quickly.

People like Tina are often more successful because they aim high, while people like Sam just squeak by. Since Tina challenges herself to do the best job she can, her career will probably be more rewarding than Sam's.

High achievers don't avoid risks, but they don't leap without looking first. Successful people learn more about what the risk involves--the potential benefits and possible losses. They then weigh the risk vs. the reward.

See each statement and debrief for an example of risk and an explanation.

Risk (Gina)

"I think trading stocks on the Internet sounds neat. I don't know a lot about the stock market, but how hard can it be? My stockbroker isn't that smart. I'm going to start investing online. I'm sure things will work out."

Debrief (Gina)

Gina isn't taking a calculated risk--she's making a foolish decision. She hasn't investigated the ups and downs of trading stocks online. Gina doesn't even know anything about the financial industry.

Risk (Carl)

"I've done a great deal of reading about trading stocks online. It can save me a great deal of money. I'll research each company before I buy or sell stock. I want to be fully informed before I take a leap."

Debrief (Carl)

Carl is taking a calculated risk. He knows the potential benefits and losses. Carl is gathering information before he takes a step, instead of jumping blindly like Gina. It's highly likely that Carl will do better financially than Gina.

People like Carl, who are high achievers, don't just settle for the information that lands on their desks. Instead, Carl looks for new developments and trends that may affect his career. Since he works in technology, he stays up to date in a variety of ways.

See each of Carl's information-gathering techniques to learn more.

Reading

"I do a lot of reading. I read trade magazines to stay up to date on technology and on my competitors. That way, I know about new products ahead of time."

Talking to clients

"I've developed a professional network to help me stay in touch. That way, I have the benefit of knowing what others hear and think about developing technology."

High achievers aren't satisfied when they meet the goals they've set for themselves. They're always looking for ways to improve. Feedback is an important part of the improvement process.

High achievers actively seek feedback. They don't avoid negative information about themselves. They seek input, then seek to correct behavior.

Jennifer is a high achiever. She is asking her boss, Brent, for feedback.

Jennifer: I'd like to get some feedback about my performance.

Brent: Well, generally, I'm pretty happy with your work. I wish everyone

Jennifer: I'm glad to hear I'm doing well. But I'd like some feedback about how I can improve. What would you like to see me do differently?

Brent: It's great that you want to improve. I guess I'd like it if you were better at anticipating customer needs. That's an area everyone can improve in.

Jennifer: Could you give me some examples? It's an area I'd like to work on, but I need some help from you.

Question

Practice what you've learned. What are the traits of individuals who continually strive for excellence?

Options:

1. They find ways to improve their performance.
2. They look for ways to track their success.
3. They actively look for new information.
4. They overlook negative feedback.
5. They set easily achieved goals for themselves.

Answer:

Actually, excellence involves looking for ways to improve, tracking success, and seeking new information.

Successful employees seek out all feedback and set strong goals.

Option 1: This answer is correct. Individuals who continually strive for excellence find ways to improve their performance because they are not satisfied with just getting by. They challenge themselves to do the best job they can.

Option 2: This answer is correct. Someone who continually strives for excellence looks for ways to track their success. By staying on top of what they are doing to be successful, they will continue to move ahead.

Option 3: This answer is correct. Individuals who strive for excellence actively look for new information. They look for new developments that may affect their careers, and they stay up to date with trends in their industry.

Option 4: This answer is incorrect. Striving for excellence doesn't mean that you overlook negative feedback, it means that you learn from it.

Option 5: This answer is incorrect. Striving for excellence means that you don't set goals that are easy to achieve, but ones that challenge you to improve.

If you want to be successful, you can learn from the behavior of other high achievers. Career-savvy workers take calculated risks and constantly scan their environment for new and relevant information.

Those who perform well constantly strive to do better. They set challenging goals. They seek feedback from others and change their behavior.

"We're all shareholders," says Tom, a worker at a large automotive plant. "Where I work, everyone has input into the process. They consider all of our opinions. And we all share rewards when the company does well."

A company that considers its employees to be shareholders often has the most committed employees. Why does this type of loyalty matter?

Loyalty and commitment benefit both the company and the individual employees. Workers feel more motivated and the company feels the result of this dedication. You will learn that when employees feel committed, they:
- are inspired by the company's mission,
- make sacrifices to meet goals,
- integrate company values into their work,
- seek opportunities to meet the group's goals.

Stacy works for a food manufacturing company that aims to improve its customers' health by making low-cost, vitamin-rich products. For Stacy, her work isn't just a job, it's a cause she cares about. She feels good about her career because she's part of a company that makes a positive impact. Stacy has high morale, which is contagious. She helps improve the attitude of other employees as well.

Employees like Stacy are willing to work hard for a cause they care about. She's likely to make personal sacrifices to meet goals. Because her company's mission is clear, it's easy for her to buy in. She can see the benefits of her loyalty.

Commitment to the company's mission can have a dramatic effect on the employee's day-to-day behavior. Employees like Stacy are often willing to make personal sacrifices to meet goals. They also integrate the goals of the company into their behavior. The company's goals are a part of their behavior pattern.

See each aspect to find out what Stacy has to say about integrating commitment into her job.

Personal Sacrifice

"I don't mind working long hours to meet our corporate goals. I think these goals matter--they make the world a better place. I also know that my employer rewards people for hard work, so it's easy to make a short-term sacrifice."

Integrating Goals

"The company goals are part of my daily work. I know quality is important to our products, so I make sure everything I do is right the first time. I try to be as efficient as possible, so I can help keep prices low."

Megan is talking with Tyler, a plant manager, about the importance of employee commitment.

an: You've told me employee commitment is important. What behaviors tell you an employee is committed?

Tyler: Well, there are a lot of ways, but one important characteristic is that the employee looks for ways to meet our goals.

Megan: So you're saying that the employee goes beyond what's expected. Can you give me an example?

Tyler: Sure. Jeremy, a worker here in the plant, looks for ways to be more efficient. He often suggests helpful process improvements.

Megan: And how do process improvements tie in to your goals?

Tyler: We look to do things inexpensively, so customers can afford our products. The more efficient we are, the lower our costs can be. Jeremy helps us watch the bottom line.

Question

Now it's your turn to practice. What are the ways that commitment benefits the company and the individual?

Options:

1. Committed employees aren't likely to share credit with their co-workers.

2. When employees are committed to their jobs, they are less likely to steal from the company.

3. Committed people spread good feelings throughout the company.

4. Committed employees usually don't "doctor" their expense accounts.

Answer:

Actually, committed employees inspire those around them. They act in an ethical manner, using company resources responsibly.

Option 1: This answer is incorrect. Being committed means that you share credit with co-workers because the entire company benefits.

Option 2: This answer is correct. Committed employees are less likely to steal from the company because they put the overall goals of the company first and the company's losing money is not one of them.

Option 3: Correct. Commitment benefits the company because committed people spread good feelings throughout the company. This high morale helps improve the attitude of other employees as well.

Option 4: This answer is correct. Commitment benefits the company because committed employees look for ways to save money, not waste money by doctoring their expense accounts.

The level of employee commitment is a key part of success for any organization. Dedicated workers will make personal sacrifices to meet a mission they can buy in to. They'll seek opportunities to meet goals.

Remember, employee commitment is a match between individual goals and company goals. Workers are loyal to companies with similar values.

How big of a part does attitude play in success? Do strong performers think differently than those who struggle?

An optimist makes the best of a bad situation. A person with initiative is moving forward, meeting goals, and making improvements in the workplace. These two components of attitude make a big difference at work. In this topic, you'll learn:

- what initiative is,
- how initiative can positively affect your career,
- what optimism is,
- why optimism is important at work.

People with initiative are ready to take advantage of opportunities. These are the people who put new ideas into place and proactively improve their workplace. They take action before problems have reached a critical stage.

Bradley, a customer service representative for an Internet service provider, is one of these people. Select each characteristic to learn how Bradley's boss feels about his initiative.

Above and Beyond

"Bradley goes above and beyond what's required. He doesn't just 'get by.' He looks for ways to improve service and find new customers. He thinks of ways to solve problems and to make life easier for everyone."

Being Proactive

"Bradley acts before he has to. If he thinks a customer isn't happy, he looks for a resolution instead of waiting for the customer to angrily call in. He knows that by cutting through red tape, he can find a solution before there's a problem."

Motivating Others

"Bradley motivates his team members to do a better job. He gets them thinking about ways to solve problems and improve their working environment. I think he's a great source of inspiration for the team."

Calm in a Crisis

"Bradley has a level head during a crisis. He focuses on solving the problem. He doesn't panic, and he doesn't get distracted by minor details. He works on solving the issue, then moving ahead with a resolution."

Optimism is all about interpretation--it's how people perceive events. Pessimistic people tend to see things in a negative, hopeless light. For these people, the glass is half empty.

Optimists tend to shed a positive light on events. They find a positive response, even in trying situations. Even optimists experience failure. The impact of failure is closely tied to how you "see" the setback. You can see the setback as confirming your worst fears, "I wasn't cut out to be a manager," or as a controllable circumstance, "Being a manager is tough. I'm going to find a mentor."

See each aspect for more information on optimism and failure.

Not Personal

An optimist sees a failure as a result of controllable factors, rather than a result of a personal flaw.

Evaluation

Optimists make a realistic evaluation of a mistake. They figure out how they contributed, and learn from their mistakes.

Your goal was to forge ahead in the face of a setback, which was a computer crash. By promoting the purchase of a new server, you can solve the problem that caused the computer crash. It's also important that you show enough initiative to meet your goals and exceed the expectations of those around you.

Question

What are the reasons why initiative and optimism are essential in work environments?

Options:

1. Optimism helps employees find positive responses to problems.

2. Initiative helps employees be proactive.

3. Optimists act from a fear of failure.

4. Optimists see mistakes as a result of a fatal flaw in themselves.

Answer:

Actually, optimism and initiative are characteristics of employees who are proactive and able to react positively in tense or negative situations.

Option 1: Correct. Optimism is essential because it helps employees find positive responses to problems because they tend to shed a positive light on events, even in trying situations.

Option 2: This answer is correct. Initiative is essential in work environments because it helps employees be proactive. Showing initiative will help to meet and exceed the expectations of those around you.

Option 3: This answer is incorrect. Pessimists, not optimists act from fear of failure. Pessimistic people tend to shed a negative light on events.

Option 4: This answer is incorrect. An optimist sees a failure as a result of controllable factors, rather than a result of a personal flaw.

Initiative and optimism are two key parts of your ability to motivate yourself. Your drive will help you find solutions before problems become serious.

If you're optimistic, you'll find a positive response to difficult situations. Your attitude toward any situation will determine your success.

CHAPTER III - EMOTIONAL INTELLIGENCE AND TEAMWORK

CHAPTER III - Emotional Intelligence and Teamwork

Participation and collaboration are key to the success of your team.

In this chapter, you'll explore the importance of these characteristics in accomplishing group goals. You'll also examine:

- the competencies needed to become an effective team member,
- the techniques for handling emotions,
- the ways to evaluate your team's emotional intelligence,
- the strategies for improving your team's emotional intelligence.

SOCIAL COMPETENCE

Social Competence

There is one thing that's true in almost every career: You'll have to work with people.

Your ability to get along with others will have a profound effect on your career, no matter what professional path you choose. In this lesson, you'll explore:
- how to show empathy for others,
- why coaching and counseling are important,
- what appreciating diversity really means.

Question

You are learning more about emotional intelligence and teamwork. What is the value of social competence?

Options:

1. You'll form positive working relationships.

2. You'll be guaranteed a raise.

3. You'll be able to get along with a wide variety of people.

4. You won't experience conflict.

Answer:

Actually, your social competence helps you form strong working relationships with a wide variety of people. Although you won't be guaranteed a raise, social competence will have a positive effect on your career.

Option 1: This is a correct answer. The value of social competence is the ability to form positive working relationships because in almost every career, you will have to work with people.

Option 2: This answer is incorrect. Social competency has to do with your ability to get along with others so it will not guarantee you a raise, but it will help you to form strong working relationships with others.

Option 3: Correct. A value of social competence is your ability to get along with a wide variety of people which will be the key to your success. Your desire to help others develop will help you accomplish your goals.

Option 4: This answer is incorrect. Social competence will not guarantee that you will not experience conflict, but it may help keep the conflict to a minimum.

As the workplace becomes increasingly globalized, your job will throw you into interactions with a wide variety of people. Your social competence abilities will be the key to your success. Your desire to help others develop will help you accomplish your goals. Empathy will assist you in building strong relationships. This lesson will provide you with the skills you need to deal with the people around you.

Mary returned to her office from a funeral. Her boss, Steve, greeted her early the morning after she returned and told her he had put some new assignments on her desk. He then quickly asked her if she could look them over and give him a timeline by noon.

Mary later complained to a co-worker, asking, "Is he even human?"

Steve isn't a robot, but he's lacking an important skill: empathy. Because he's missing this skill set, he isn't able to relate to employees like Mary effectively. In this topic, you'll explore:

- the importance of empathy,
- the effect of empathy on interactions,
- characteristics of people who are empathetic.

What happens when you don't have empathy? You'll "trip up" emotionally. Empathy is your ability to figure out what other people are feeling without being told. This understanding will aid you in determining the best way to approach your team members.

See With empathy and Without empathy for more information.

With empathy

If you have empathy, you can change your behavior when necessary. You'll read other people's feelings, then act accordingly.

Without empathy

Without empathy, you run the risk of saying inappropriate things. Like Steve, you will plunge ahead without considering other people's feelings.

Question

What happens if you don't have empathy?

Options:

1. Others see you as "cold."
2. People won't tell you about their needs.
3. You'll say the wrong thing.
4. Other people will keep their distance.
5. Relationships will seem awkward or uncomfortable.

Answer:

Actually, when you don't have empathy, other people will avoid confiding in you because they see you as indifferent. Your interactions with others will be difficult.

Option 1: This option is correct. If you don't have empathy, others will see you as cold and will have a difficult time interacting with you.

Option 2: This answer is correct. If you don't have empathy, people won't tell you about their needs. If this is the case, you will have a hard time interacting with and managing others.

Option 3: This answer is correct. If you lack empathy, you might say the wrong thing; you will plunge ahead without considering other people's feelings.

Option 4: This answer is correct. As a result of lacking empathy, other people will keep their distance because they will see you as indifferent.

Option 5: This answer is correct. Because of the lack of empathy, relationships will seem awkward or uncomfortable, which means you will have difficulty approaching team members.

People with empathy share common behaviors. They accurately read the feelings of others and they adjust their actions accordingly. Empathetic people build effective relationships because they understand other people's feelings and needs.

See each trait to learn about the characteristics of empathetic people.

Good listeners

Empathetic people are good listeners. They listen without interrupting or giving advice. These skills can be especially important when dealing with customers. The best listeners pay

attention so they meet customers' needs and desires.

Others' viewpoints

Empathetic people see things from other points of view. They are able to understand what makes another person angry, frustrated, or happy. They can put themselves in someone else's shoes.

Pick up on cues

When people have empathy, they don't just listen to words. They pick up on nonverbal cues such as tone of voice, body movement, and facial expressions. After all, people don't speak only with words.

Show sensitivity

In order to demonstrate empathy, you must show sensitivity. You shouldn't cut people off or judge what they are saying. You should be careful not to hurt other people's feelings.

Question

You work alongside Anne, an accountant. She's struggling with a new auditing process your company has implemented. You're trying your best to assist her, since the process is complicated and frustrating.

While Anne's going through this difficult time, what should you do to behave empathetically toward her? Choose all that apply.

Options:

1. You should listen to Anne's frustrations.

2. You should tell Anne that she needs to readjust her attitude.

3. You should watch Anne's nonverbal behavior.

4. You should adjust your behavior based on emotional cues you receive from Anne.

Answer:

Actually, people with empathy pay attention to the emotional cues of others and act accordingly. They are in tune with the people around them.

Option 1: This answer is correct. While Anne's going through this difficult time, you should listen to her frustrations because being empathetic means sometimes you should listen without interrupting or giving advice.

Option 2: This answer is incorrect. While Anne is going through the difficult time, you should not tell Anne that she needs to readjust her attitude because this would not be showing her empathy.

Option 3: This answer is correct. You can help Anne through this difficult time by watching her nonverbal behavior because being empathetic means you pick up on nonverbal cues such as tone of voice, body movement, and facial expressions.

Option 4: Correct. You can help Anne by adjusting your behavior based on emotional cues you receive from her. Because you are empathetic, you build effective relationships because you understand other people's feelings and needs.

Empathy is an important skill in relating to others. To have empathy for others, you must care about their feelings and make an effort to see their points of view.

Your ability to empathize will help you relate effectively to co-workers and customers. You'll be able to understand their emotions and respond to their needs.

After five years of working for Angela, Elliot knew a lot more about recruiting than when he started off. . Angela had helped him figure out his strengths and weaknesses and helped him become better at his job.

How did Angela develop and motivate Elliot?

Angela acts as a coach and a counselor for Elliot. Her management style goes beyond checking deadlines and filling out performance reviews. She helps Elliot reach for the top by giving him feedback and helping him set goals. In this lesson, you'll explore:

- the importance of coaching and counseling,
- the characteristics of effective coaches.

Jeff is a supervisor in the loan application division of a large bank. His manager and employees consider him a great coach and counselor.

See each action for Jeff's ideas about how to develop people.

Give praise

"It's important to let people know what they've done correctly. Most people receive a lot of negative feedback, but never hear praise. I always let my employees know what they've done well."

Give feedback

"I appreciate it when people give me feedback, so I try to return the favor. It's important to let people know what their development needs are. If they want to progress in their careers, they'll have to tackle areas where they need improvement."

Challenge employees

"My employees want to develop. The best way for them to develop is through challenging assignments. I try to find out the skills my workers want to build, then I look for assignments that will help them grow."

Allow goal setting

"Instead of setting goals for my employees, I let them set the direction for their own development. I want them to figure out where their careers should go. After all, they should be responsible for their own careers."

Question

Kelly and Sam are lifeguards at a beach-side resort. Sam has been on the job three years, while Kelly recently started. What are some methods Sam could use to effectively coach and counsel Kelly?

Options:

1. Sam should acknowledge Kelly's accomplishments.
2. Sam should hold off on giving Kelly feedback.
3. Sam should help Kelly set her own goals.
4. Sam should offer constructive criticism.

Answer:

Actually, Sam can best coach and counsel Kelly by giving her constructive and timely feedback. He can help by letting her know what she's done well and what behavior she can improve.

Option 1: This answer is correct. This is an effective coaching method. Sam should acknowledge Kelly's accomplishments because it is important to let her know that he recognizes and appreciates what she has done correctly.

Option 2: This answer is incorrect. Sam should not hold off providing Kelly feedback because his coaching will be most effective when it is timely.

Option 3: This answer is correct. In order to effectively coach and counsel Kelly, Sam should help her set goals because it's important that she be responsible for her own career.

Option 4: This answer is correct. In order to effectively coach and counsel Kelly, Sam should offer constructive criticism because then she will understand areas where she needs improvement.

Your coaching and counseling skills will help you develop your co-workers and employees. You can take the opportunity to acknowledge other people's strengths and accomplishments.

You can also assist others by providing feedback and helping them set development goals.

Phil, the director of a financial planning firm hired Jackie, thinking she would bring in more female clients.

Once she joined the firm, he realized what a mistake he'd been making all along before hiring Jackie. Phil realized that everyone who worked at the firm was the same, like a bunch of clones. Bringing Jackie on board was a great move. She took a totally different approach, which has helped expand the client base.

Phil has learned how to value diversity. Initially, he hired a woman because he thought he "should." Now he's learned that diversity can be more than just a surface-level advantage. You'll examine:

- how stereotypes can prevent you from getting along with others,
- what's needed to get along with a wide variety of people,
- how a diverse work force can add value.

Question

Stereotypes are prevalent in society. Which of the following statements are stereotypes?

Options:

1. Women care more about getting married than building a career.
2. Caucasian people are bad dancers.
3. Hispanic people are lazy.
4. People of the Jewish faith have a lot of money.
5. Men don't have emotions.
6. Catholics have a lot of children.

Answer:

Actually, these are all stereotypes. While some are more common than others, they are generalizations that do not apply to every member of the selected group.

Option 1: This choice is correct. That women care more about getting married than building a career is a stereotype because it is a generalization that does not apply to all women.

Option 2: This option is correct. This is a stereotype because it generalizes Caucasians as a race of bad dancers.

Option 3: This answer is correct. The stereotype that Hispanic people are lazy does not take into account the percentage of the race that is hard working and dedicated.

Option 4: This answer is correct. That people of the Jewish faith have a lot of money is a stereotype. Not only does it generalize based on ethnicity, but it also projects an image that may only be true in some cases.

Option 5: This is correct option. That men don't have emotions is a generalization, which makes it a stereotype because it does not apply to all men.

Option 6: This answer is correct. Catholics have a lot of children is a stereotype because the statement generalizes to all members of the religious group that which is only true of some.

You have probably heard a stereotype about every ethnic group, gender, age group, and religion. These generalizations can affect relationships, clouding the way people see each other.

Maria used to work for a law firm, where she experienced some frustrations. Daniel asked his co-worker Maria about the stereotypes she experienced at the law firm.

Maria: I think there were a lot of stereotypes because I'm a woman and I'm Hispanic.

Daniel: How do you think those stereotypes affected your work environment? Were people hostile?

Maria: They weren't hostile, but they made a lot of assumptions. For instance, they sent all the female clients to me.

Daniel: Was it a problem to work with a female-only client base?

Maria: It wasn't a problem because they were women, but just because a client was female, they assumed I had the expertise to deal with her case. That wasn't always true.

Daniel: Did you experience problems because of your Hispanic origin?

Maria: Yes. They assumed that I wanted to work on any "ethnic" cases that came up. But actually, my background is in corporate law and most of the cases weren't relevant.

Maria's firm was not taking advantage of diversity. She wasn't given work based on her skills--she was assigned work based on her gender and race.

Maria now works for another firm in which diversity is celebrated. Maria's boss, Will, gets along well with his employees who come from a variety of backgrounds.

See each action for Maria's comments about how Will gets along with a diverse mix of employees.

Shows respect

"Will has a lot of respect for people and their abilities. You can tell he values us all. He's pleasant, has empathy for the situations others face, and seeks to make the work environment agreeable for everyone."

Challenges biases

"Will expects all of us to respect each other. He doesn't allow stereotyping or bias to exist. When someone makes generalizations about a race, gender, or age group, he's the first person to challenge that kind of talk."

Sees diversity as opportunity

"Will sees diversity as an opportunity. He feels that we can all learn from the experiences and viewpoints we bring to the team. He doesn't want a cookie-cutter work force--he wants a team that reflects the real world."

Judges accurately

"Will judges people accurately. He evaluates based on skill and performance, without letting stereotypes cloud his view. We all face the same expectations no matter what our age, race, gender, or religion is."

A diverse work force isn't important just because of legal requirements. An employee base that brings together many types of people can be a strong advantage in today's global work force.

See each business factor for Maria's comments about the advantages of diversity.

knowledge and perspective

"A blended work force brings the knowledge and background of many types of people together. The more diverse your employees are, the more perspectives you will be able to blend. You'll have the advantage of a variety of sources of information and expertise."

learning throughout the company

"When new people come onto the team, it's an opportunity for everyone to learn. The more diverse the group, the greater the opportunity for growth. Employees can learn more about their customers and competitors from the people on their team."

new directions

"When teams diversify, new opportunities are often discovered. By bringing a fresh perspective, new members may be able to think of new products, services, or ways to treat customers. A static work force often can't develop in this way."

adaptability

"The more your work team reflects the world outside, the better prepared it will be to face business changes. Employees from a wide variety of backgrounds can come up with new processes and responses to marketplace changes."

Question

Now, practice what you've learned. What are some characteristics of people who deal well with diversity?

Options:

1. They avoid stereotyping people.

2. They see diversity as an opportunity.

3. They see people from different backgrounds as having different levels of skill.

4. They see diversity in the workplace as a burden.

Answer:

Actually, people who deal well with diversity are sensitive to the differences between people, but avoid stereotyping. They see diversity as a learning opportunity.

Option 1: This is a correct choice. One characteristic of people who deal well with diversity is they avoid stereotyping people because the use of these types of generalizations can affect relationships, and cloud the way people see each other.

Option 2: This answer is correct. People who deal well with diversity see it as an opportunity because it brings the knowledge and background of many types of people together and will often lead to new directions and discoveries.

Option 3: This answer is incorrect. This is not a characteristic of diversity because even individuals with the same backgrounds have different levels of skills.

Option 4: This choice is incorrect. Seeing diversity in the workplace as a burden is a characteristic of someone who does not deal well with diversity, otherwise they would see it as an opportunity for the company.

In order to be socially competent in the workplace, you must be able to deal with a wide variety of people. The work force is changing rapidly and you'll need to shed outdated stereotypes in order to take advantage of opportunities.

By valuing the diversity you encounter, you'll be able to build strong business partnerships. Your respect for others will be an advantage.

INFLUENCING OTHERS

Influencing Others

What does it take to influence other people? Does it take power..or luck? Or are there skills that play into a person's ability to influence?

It's a common misconception that influence and power go hand in hand. Many people have strong influencing skills without the benefit of a large office or an important title. Other people make it into highly visible positions without understanding how to motivate others. These people will have a difficult time in leadership roles if they don't develop influencing ability.

This lesson will cover the skills you need to influence the people around you. It's not necessary to be in a power position to exert influence over others. It's a matter of skill, not authority.

You'll examine methods of persuasion and learn what it takes to be an effective communicator. You will also explore the importance of conflict management.

Melissa thinks her company should institute a telecommuting policy. However, it would be a big change for the company. How can she convince her boss to give telecommuting a try?

Persuasion is an emotional ability. If Melissa wants to convince her boss, she'll need to use a wide range of skills, including reading his emotions, understanding his motivations, and listening to his emotional cues. She'll also need an understanding of the strategies that can be used to persuade someone. Melissa will have to pick the most effective methods for persuading her boss.

Persuasion can involve logic. After all, Melissa won't persuade her boss unless she produces evidence concerning the advantages of telecommuting. However, Melissa will also need to appeal to her boss emotionally. He'll be more convinced if he is emotionally persuaded.

See each action for more information about emotion and persuasion.

Arousing emotions

Persuasion hinges on arousing emotions in another person. People with this ability know that they have to appeal to what the listener cares about.

Appealing to emotions

Persuaders often appeal to a person's respect for power, excitement about a project, desire to outdo a competitor, or outrage concerning an injustice.

There are many emotional skills Melissa should have before she attempts to persuade her boss. See each technique to learn more about the competencies that factor into persuasion.

empathy

Good persuaders have empathy for their audience. They understand what motivates the people they're trying to persuade. For instance, Melissa knows her boss is concerned about overhead and turnover. If she can target these issues, she'll have a better chance of success.

rapport

Strong persuaders build rapport with their listeners. They get along well with the audience. Melissa must be able to have a pleasant conversation with her boss before she can convince him. She should build a casual relationship before pushing her agenda.

indirect influence

Indirect influence is a way of getting someone else to convince the target audience. Melissa could provide her boss with magazine articles and other reports about telecommuting. The evidence might convince him.

emotional cues

It's important to be able to read emotional cues. If Melissa brings up telecommuting and her boss looks uncomfortable, he may have a concern she needs to address. If Melissa misses subtle signals like this, she may offend the person she's trying to convince.

adapting to the audience

Good persuaders always know when to switch their tactic. If the target audience isn't responding, the method of persuasion needs to change. If Melissa makes a presentation that doesn't go over well, she should switch to a different tactic.

It's important to use a variety of methods in the persuasion process. Everyone is unique and will be convinced by different approaches. Ted sells air conditioning units to wholesalers. He uses a wide range of persuasion techniques with his customers.

See each technique for some strategies Ted uses.

Logical Appeals

"I often use facts and figures to persuade customers. I use pricing charts, warranty information, and product specifications. These help the customer see the benefits of using my products."

Dramatic Appeals

"One time I couldn't convince a supplier by using price sheets or product specifications. So, I went to his office and installed a sample product. When he saw how well my unit worked, he switched to my product."

Building Support

"I can also build support within the customer's company. I meet people at trade shows and demonstrate my product. If they like it, they'll help convince their managers to buy it."

Managing Impressions

"My customers work in warehouses. If I show up in a suit, they'll think I'm an idiot. I dress like them. I work to answer even the most obscure product questions, so they feel confident about my advice."

Question

Practice what you've learned. What are some effective strategies used in persuasion? Choose all that apply.

Options:

1. emotional appeals
2. logical appeals
3. using half-truths
4. impression management
5. dramatic appeals

Answer:

Actually, a wide range of strategies including emotional, logical, and dramatic appeals, and impression management are used in persuasion. However, half-truths are not a recommended strategy.

Option 1: This answer is correct. One effective strategy used in persuasion is emotional appeals. Because persuasion hinges on arousing emotions in another person you must know what the listener cares about.

Option 2: This choice is correct. Appealing to logic is an effective strategy used in persuasion because using facts and figures is often the most basic way to win someone over.

Option 3: This answer is incorrect. Lying or telling half-truths is not an effective strategy because the consequences of being caught rarely outweigh the benefits gained from being dishonest.

Option 4: This answer is correct. Impression management is an effective strategy used in persuasion. It means you understand your audience and appeal to their needs, be it your boss, co-worker, or customer.

Option 5: This answer is correct. Dramatic appeals can be a very effective persuasion strategies because often times you will have more success showing than simply telling.

Remember, persuasion is a combination of appeals to logic and emotion. Effective persuaders are able to empathize with their audience and understand what will be most convincing.

Effective approaches blend a wide range of strategies, including indirect influence, emotional appeals, logical appeals, and impression management.

Grant, a project coordinator, had been working for Shannon for three years. He never heard her give any positive feedback or the least bit of encouragement and felt she was very hard to work for.

Shannon would simply ignore her staff unless she needed something. Grant decided that anyone that distant could not be an effective leader.

Shannon will have to improve her communication before she can become an effective leader. She can build a strong foundation by working on her listening skills.

Shannon can also become a better communicator by using a blend of skills, including fostering open communication, controlling her emotions, and being straightforward.

Self-control is an important part of communication. When someone gets carried away by bad moods or upsetting events, they aren't fully available to the people around them.

See each worker for examples of self-control.

Robert

Robert sometimes seems moody and distant. He often snaps at people or lashes out. People avoid him because they're not sure how he's going to behave.

Dana

Dana is always cool and composed, even in bad situations. She never flies off the handle or acts like she's not paying attention.

Question

Listening effectively is a part of good communication. To respond and react appropriately, you have to understand the other person's input. Which of the following behaviors contribute to good listening?

Options:

1. asking perceptive questions

2. paying attention to distractions
3. having empathy
4. asking for suggestions
5. interrupting
6. being open-minded

Answer:

Actually, good listeners ask astute questions. They're open-minded, receptive to feedback, and have empathy. They avoid distractions and don't interrupt the speaker.

Option 1: This answer is correct. Part of good listening is asking perceptive questions because this shows you are paying attention to the person speaking and you understand their issues and concerns.

Option 2: This answer is incorrect. Paying attention to distractions is not a part of effective communication because it implies you are not paying attention to the speaker.

Option 3: This answer is correct. Having empathy contributes to good listening because it means you understand what the other person is going through.

Option 4: This answer is correct. Asking for suggestions contributes to good listening because it indicates your value the other person's input and opinion.

Option 5: This answer is incorrect. Interrupting does not lead to good listening because it signifies a lack of interest.

Option 6: This answer is correct. Being open-minded contributes to good listening because it shows you are willing to deal with all types of issues.

How can Shannon improve her communication style? To begin with, she should work on her listening skills. She should also avoid letting her moods interfere in her interactions.

See each tactic for some other behaviors Shannon should work on.

Be Open

Shannon should be open to all kinds of information--both good and bad. She should be receptive to other people's feedback. This openness fosters communication. Employees will be more likely to tell her about problems before they become crises.

Share Information

Shannon should share more information. She should communicate about accomplishments and other news instead of just handing out assignments and negative feedback. Her employees will feel more connected through frequent communication.

Be Straightforward

Shannon should be straightforward when a difficult issue arises. She should explain problems without becoming emotional. She shouldn't hide bad news or try to cover up problems. Honesty will build trust.

Build Understanding

Shannon needs to make sure other people understand her messages. Likewise, she should try to understand the communication she receives. She should spend time talking to employees to ensure that an understanding has been built.

Question

Practice what you've learned. Identify some effective methods of communication.

Options:

1. tailoring the message based on emotional cues

2. avoiding negative feedback
3. remaining calm
4. building mutual understanding
5. listening carefully

Answer:

Actually, effective communication involves good listening and building understanding. It's important to remain calm and consider all information, even negative feedback.

Option 1: Correct. One effective method of communication is to tailor the message based on emotional cues. Active listening and reading non-verbal behavior will provide you clues to a person's emotional state.

Option 2: This answer is incorrect. Effective communication does not mean avoiding negative feedback because hiding bad news or covering up problems will not build trust.

Option 3: This answer is correct. Remaining calm is an effective method of communication because it indicates you can handle even the most difficult situation rationally and with self-control.

Option 4: This choice is correct. Building mutual understanding is an effective method of communication because it means taking the time to understand others and ensuring messages are clear.

Option 5: This answer is correct. Listening carefully is an effective method of communication because good listening shows that you care what the other person has to say and that you are open to other's ideas.

Shannon can improve her communication style. The first step is understanding the importance of effective

communication. She can also integrate the following behaviors:
- remaining calm,
- being a good listener,
- building mutual understanding,
- sharing information,
- fostering open communication,
- being straightforward about difficult information.

Sean needs to talk to his co-worker, Heidi, about the noise level in the office. She's constantly on the phone, making it difficult for him to concentrate. How can he talk to her without causing a scene?

There is a four-step model Sean can use to manage his conflict situation. This process won't help him avoid conflict altogether, but it will help him manage the disagreement. The steps in the model are:
- Express your feelings.
- Show a willingness to work together to find a solution.
- State your viewpoint calmly.
- Work as a team to find a solution.

Managing a conflict effectively requires self-control and a willingness to work with other people. If Sean becomes demanding or hostile, his conversation with Heidi probably won't be productive.

See each action for more information.

Express feelings

Sean should express his feelings without becoming emotional, or making a personal attack. He should use "I" statements like, "I'm frustrated" instead of "you" statements like, "You're too loud."

Show willingness to work together

Sean should show a desire to work with Heidi to find a solution. He should be open to talking about the problem and her concerns. He should encourage an open discussion.

State viewpoint calmly

Sean should state his point of view calmly. He should ask for the changes he'd like to see, without becoming hostile or demanding. Sean should feel free to request changes but should not become angry if Heidi hesitates to comply.

Work as a team

Sean should avoid telling Heidi what to do or how to change her behavior. Instead, they should discuss a solution together. They may need to reach a compromise in which they both give up small things to reach a mutually satisfactory conclusion.

Sean talked to Heidi about the noise level in the office.

Sean: Heidi, I'm concerned about the noise level in the office. I prefer to work in a quiet environment.

Heidi: So, are you saying that you don't want me to use the phone anymore? Because I do have to make some calls to the branch office. Those calls are pretty important.

Sean: I'm not asking you to stop doing your job. I'd like to work together to find a solution that's effective for both of us.

Heidi: Well, we do have to share this office indefinitely. Do you have any ideas?

Sean: I don't think it's possible to be totally quiet. But I'd like to set aside a few hours each day for quiet work time.

Heidi: I suppose I could save all my calls for the afternoon.

Sean: I don't want to inconvenience you. But, if we could set aside a three- hour block, I'd really appreciate it.

Heidi: Let's look at our schedules and see if we can figure something out.

Sean stayed calm while he talked to Heidi. She was tense at first, but began to relax as the conversation moved forward. Sean clearly explained the problem and told Heidi why the noise level was a concern. He was open to working with her to find a solution, instead of making demands. If Sean acted angry or overbearing, Heidi could have gotten upset quickly, and he might have ended up with a bigger problem than he started with.

Your goal is to work as a team to find a solution to a group problem. This approach will yield the best results.

Question

Practice what you've learned. You're a software trainer who is expected to share weekend training classes with another instructor, Ashley. She hasn't taught a Saturday or Sunday class in over a month. You're frustrated because you'd like to have an occasional weekend off. What strategies should you use to resolve this conflict with Ashley?

Options:

1. You should express your feelings about working weekends.

2. You should be as aggressive as possible with Ashley.

3. You should state your viewpoint calmly.

4. You should work with Ashley to find a mutually agreeable solution.

Answer:

Actually, you should communicate openly and honestly with Ashley, but avoid being aggressive or confrontational. You should work with her to find a solution.

Option 1: Correct. Expressing your feelings about working weekends is a strategy you should use to resolve your conflict with Ashley. You should do so without becoming emotional, or making a personal attack, which will help Ashley open up to your ideas.

Option 2: This answer is incorrect. Being aggressive with Ashley will not help to resolve the conflict because that will only serve to put her on the defensive and you may end up with a bigger problem than you started with.

Option 3: This answer is correct. Another strategy is to state your viewpoint calmly and discuss the weekend issue without becoming hostile or demanding. You should not become angry if Ashley hesitates to comply.

Option 4: This answer is correct. In order to solve the conflict, you should work with Ashley to find a mutually agreeable solution. You may need to reach a compromise in which you both give up small things to reach a mutually satisfactory conclusion.

Remember, aggression is not the key to dealing with conflict. The best approach is a method in which you work as a team with others to solve the problem. You will need to work through a process of give and take to find a resolution that works for everyone.

Your ability to remain calm and focused, instead of becoming emotional, is your best weapon in conflict. Keep in mind--conflict should not become personal. Remain neutral and open to suggestions.

PARTICIPATION AND COLLABORATION

Participation and Collaboration
"The way a team plays as a whole determines its success. You may have the greatest bunch of individual stars in the world, but if they don't play together, the club won't be worth a dime." --Babe Ruth

Have you ever been on a team that didn't work well together? Ultimately, these groups become frustrating for everyone involved. Goals don't get accomplished and team members are alienated.

Participation and collaboration are essential to building a team in which the members work well together. Without these key ingredients, you won't have a team--you'll have individual players.

Question
What behaviors make the difference in building teams?
Options:
1. building strong relationships
2. creating goals that are shared among team members
3. competition among group members

4. good group chemistry
Answer:
Actually, strong relationships, good chemistry, and shared goals are key ingredients to strong team relationships. Competition only serves to separate group members.

Option 1: This answer is correct. One element in team building is strong relationships because without good relationships, you will not get what you need or find support when you encounter problems.

Option 2: Correct. Creating shared goals makes the difference in team building because if the team members share the same goals, they're likely to work well together.

Option 3: This answer is incorrect. Competition among group members is not an element of team building because competition only serves to separate group members.

Option 4: This answer is correct. Good group chemistry makes the difference in building teams. Effective teams have fewer problems with turnover and absenteeism. Productivity rises.

You'll examine ways to foster key connections within the team to help create and attain shared goals. You'll also gain insight into what factors contribute to team synergy.

You'll see the characteristics that help build teams that work, rather than groups that struggle.

Have you ever heard of an "old boys' network?" This is an informal group of people that controls a given industry. Have these behind-the-scenes power structures disappeared?

The old boys' network may have fallen out of favor in today's business environment. However, powerful, informal connections still exist in most organizations today. People rely on their network of relationships within their company and industry to find jobs, project funding, and other important resources.

You'll examine the importance of professional associations to your career success. You'll also explore ways to effectively build links to key players in your business environment.

How can relationships make a difference in your career? The network you build can provide opportunities such as jobs, promotions, and exciting projects. These associations can provide relief during stressful times as well.

See each business situation for some examples of how your connections can have an effect.

Customer order

"A customer asked for a larger order at the last minute. It was a great opportunity, but I didn't have the supplies on hand. We've worked with the same vendor for years. I called him up and he came through for me."

Job loss

"I found out that my division was cutting back and that I would lose my job. I have a great relationship with a manager in another department. He found a place for me right away. It's turned out to be a great career opportunity."

Technical problem

"We'd almost finished our project when three of our computers went down. I've done several favors for the manager in the technical support division. When I called during the crisis, he came right over and resolved our problem."

Admin support

"I have a great relationship with the support people in our office. They're under a lot of pressure, so it's hard for them to meet everyone's needs. But they always seem to come through for me. I think it's because they consider me a friend."

Good business depends on good relationships. Today's work world is getting more complex all the time. It's likely that there are parts of your job you can't do alone. You probably need information, guidance, or support from other people, departments, and businesses.

If you don't build good relationships with the people you interact with, you'll probably run into dead ends. You won't get what you need, or you won't find support when you encounter problems.

What can you do to foster good relationships in the workplace? It all starts with treating people the way that you'd like to be treated. You need to be conscious of the interactions that take place in your work world.

Read about each technique to find out how you can nurture your informal network:

making "useful" friendships

Useful friendships are mutually beneficial. You may know people within your company and industry who can help you. The odds are that you can provide assistance to these same people. These mutually beneficial relationships are a strong link in your professional network.

being cooperative

You probably have the opportunity to do favors for other people. Consider helping others out, especially if you know they may be in a position to assist you in the future. This applies to people above and below you in rank, as well as vendors and suppliers.

building rapport

Building rapport is an ongoing process. Have casual conversations with people in your office about subjects that aren't work-related. Attend networking and social functions so you can get to know others better. Make an effort to meet new faces.

sharing information

It can be extremely frustrating to be "out of the loop." People are grateful to those who share important information. Take the time to communicate relevant issues to co-workers, vendors, and other departments.

keeping a balance

Professional friendships are very important to your success. Keep in mind that you must avoid clashes in these relationships. Resist the urge to gossip or become involved in personal conflicts that take place at work. This behavior can damage the network you've worked to build.

Question

Practice what you've learned. Identify the techniques for nurturing instrumental relationships.

Options:

1. allowing overlaps between your personal and professional life
2. having casual conversations with co-workers
3. steering clear of friendships at work
4. avoiding networking opportunities

Answer:

Actually, it's important to build relationships within the workplace. You can do this by taking the opportunity to interact with people in your office and in your industry.

Option 1: Correct. In order to nurture instrumental relationships allow overlaps between your personal and professional life. This network will benefit you in both good and bad times.

Option 2: Correct. Because nurturing instrumental relationships is an ongoing process, have casual conversations with people in your office about subjects that are not work-related. This effort will build useful relationships for you to rely on in the future.

Option 3: This answer is incorrect. If you steer clear of friendships at work you will not nurture instrumental relationships because you will not be able to easily find the assistance or resources you need.

Option 4: This answer is incorrect. By avoiding networking opportunities, you will miss the opportunity to find jobs, project funding, and nurture other important resources and relationships.

Your professional network will benefit you in both good and bad times. You can look to your colleagues for help when you're struggling. However, these relationships are reciprocal. Do your part to help others and you'll be strengthening connections in your industry.

Paul thought that Sharon didn't show the least bit of respect for him or what he did.

He felt that all she cared about was getting what she wanted when she wanted it. He complained that she talked to him like he was her servant. Paul decided that he couldn't care less about Sharon's priorities and that he wasn't going to break his neck to get her work done.

Is Paul being unreasonable? Or is Sharon's management style the real problem? Both could use some work, but Paul would probably change his attitude if

Sharon treated him differently. Sharon needs to think about the following points:
- the importance of creating shared goals,
- what happens when goals aren't supported by everyone,
- ways to get buy-in.

Question

What happens when everyone does not share the same goals? There are a lot of potential ramifications. What could Paul do to sabotage Sharon?

Options:

1. Paul could miss deadlines.

2. Paul could make intentional mistakes.

3. Paul might try to make Sharon look bad in front of her boss or a customer.

4. Paul may not do the best he can on Sharon's work, lowering the quality of the end-product.

Answer:

Actually, Paul could do all these things to "get back" at Sharon.

Option 1: This answer is correct. Because Paul and Sharon don't share the same goals, Paul might miss deadlines in order to sabotage Sharon. Sharon needs to remember that she relies on Paul to help her look good.

Option 2: This answer is correct. In order to sabotage Sharon, Paul could make intentional mistakes. Because they don't share the same goals they work against one another.

Option 3: This answer is correct. To sabotage Sharon, Paul might try to make her look bad in front of her boss or a customer. Because they don't share the same goals, Paul works against her instead of with her, which makes Sharon look bad.

Option 4: This answer is correct. Because they don't share the same goals, Paul has no reason to work hard for Sharon. He may not do the best he can on Sharon's work, lowering the quality of the end-product.

The conflict between Paul and Sharon is an example of a situation in which an employee doesn't share management or department goals. Not all examples are this drastic, but unpleasant effects can still exist. The bottom line is that every manager depends on his employees to make him look good to his customers and his boss. The employees in turn depend on the manager for raises, performance reviews, and promotions.

If the employee and the manager share the same goals, they're likely to work well together. But if a supervisor sets goals that don't make sense to workers, trouble may ensue.

There are four techniques that you can use to create shared goals. These tools all share one common theme: Have respect and empathy for the people you work with. By keeping their needs and interests in mind, you'll take the first step toward a good relationship.

See each technique to find out more about creating shared goals.

Keep the relationship in mind

It's easy to get caught up in tasks. However, it's important that you keep your team relationship in mind. Don't just think about finishing the job. Consider how you can work with the other person effectively. Keep their needs and pressures in mind.

Work as a team

Teams share information and resources. They communicate their plans to others. Surprises aren't always a good thing at work. Talk to your co-workers. Communicate ideas and listen to other people's input. Work to get the job done without making relationships go sour.

Create a cooperative environment

It's difficult to cooperate and compete at the same time. Encourage people to work together to accomplish goals. Support people who help their co-workers when they're struggling. Be friendly to others and treat people with respect.

Look for opportunities

Seek out opportunities to get input from other people and departments. Have people work on projects that you know they're interested in. Help people develop the skills they need to contribute to team projects. Don't wait for people to ask for development opportunities.

Sharon is going to work on her relationship with Paul. She's learned how to create shared goals and she's committed to changing her behavior.

See how Sharon worked toward improving the goal-sharing process with Paul.

Sharon: I know I haven't taken the time to get your input on projects in the past. I'm afraid I've seemed abrupt, and I'd like to work toward a different relationship.

Paul: It's tough for me because I work for several people. I can't anticipate all of your needs or figure out how you want things done.

Sharon: That makes sense. Let's try a different approach for the next project. Could we sit down and talk about the client and what kind of work we'll need to do?

Paul: It would certainly help if we planned ahead a little. It's easier for me to juggle projects if I know what lies ahead.

Sharon: I can tell you what needs I'll probably have. Then you could tell me what kind of timelines work for you. I won't just throw deadlines at you anymore. You'll build the schedule and I'll respect it.

Paul: That would be wonderful. It would take a lot of pressure off of me. Sharon: Is there anything else I could do to make things easier? I don't want to seem like the bullheaded manager. I want you to enjoy your work.

Paul: Well, it would be great if I could have a lunch hour to myself, instead of being forced to work through it. I'd rather come in early than miss that break--it really refreshes me.

Sharon laid the foundation for building a better relationship with Paul. Instead of dumping assignments on him, she's working with him to set a schedule. Paul will be responsible for setting his own goals instead of taking on a timeline set by Sharon. She's also fostering an open communication environment by actively seeking his feedback about her work style. It's important for Sharon to stick by these commitments so that Paul sees the actual behavior change.

Question
Practice what you've learned. Choose the methods for creating shared goals.

Options:
1. Show faith in the other person's abilities.

2. Clarify roles.
3. Share information.
4. Carefully control other peoples' work.

Answer:

Actually, to create shared goals, it's important to build a positive, nurturing relationship with others. This includes showing confidence, clarifying responsibilities, and sharing information.

Option 1: This answer is correct. Creating shared goals means showing faith in the other person's abilities. If you don't trust and respect other people you work with, you won't have a solid foundation you can rely on.

Option 2: Correct. Clarifying roles will help to create shared goals because each person will know and buy into their piece of the project. You should identify roles early into the assignment or project so everyone understands their responsibilities.

Option 3: This answer is correct. To create shared goals, you should share information and work like a team. By communicating ideas and listening to other people's input, the job will get done without making relationships go sour.

Option 4: This answer is incorrect. Controlling other people's work is not a method for creating shared goals because it shows that you don't trust or respect their ability to get the job done. This is likely to foster resentment from the others.

When employees and managers don't share goals, serious problems can develop. Employees can sabotage projects and profits. Managers can derail careers. It's important that everyone is a team, working toward the same goal.

The foundation for good relationships is an atmosphere of trust and confidence in the abilities of others. Setting team goals can make a difference in quality and productivity.

"Coming together is a beginning, staying together is progress, and working together is success." --Henry Ford

The chemistry a team possesses determines its success or failure. This explains why some groups flourish, while others struggle. You'll explore:
- the reasons teams are popular
- the importance of group synergy
- the characteristics that create synergy.

Work teams are becoming increasingly popular. Why? Because the business world is changing. As customer needs change and technology increases possibilities, workers are constantly shifting job responsibilities. Few people can expect to do the same job and work with the same people, year after year. Many teams are pulled together for a single project, then disbanded after completion.

Many people like working with a good team. Effective teams have fewer problems with turnover and absenteeism. Productivity rises. Teams provide a lot of benefits when they're running well.

Not all goals can be evenly split into manageable tasks. It takes more than a division of labor to complete most projects. This is where team synergy comes into play.

Select Synergy is and Workplace tasks for more information.

Synergy is...

Synergy is the action of two or more people to achieve an effect which each person is individually incapable of achieving.

Workplace tasks

Workplace tasks are becoming more complicated. Most of them can't be done alone or split evenly into tasks. Group synergy is needed to accomplish goals.

The team members shown work for a furniture manufacturing company. They're working hard to get a new product line produced and marketed by the beginning of next year. The team is on track with a superior product. How are they doing it? The group has great synergy.

See each team component for more information on the characteristics of group synergy.

Facts

"We all communicate openly with each other. I don't feel like anyone is hiding information. It's great because I always know the important facts and I feel like people who share information are committed to our goal."

Roles

"I think the team members work in roles that match their talents. It's most effective that way. No one is struggling to do his job, and we each spend our time with tasks that we like."

Empathy

"Everyone on this team has empathy for each other. We respect our co-workers and we care about the problems they're facing. I like the fact that the environment isn't critical or destructive. We build each other up, instead of cutting one another down."

Relationships

"Our team has to build effective relationships with other teams in the organization. This small team has its own goals, but we have to remember that our goals support the company goals. We can't treat other teams as enemies."

Goals

"We have a very clear goal. We all know what we're out to accomplish, so it's easy to stay focused. I've worked on teams with unclear missions--it's like trying to hit a moving target. It's very frustrating."

Flexibility

"The team members have worked hard to be flexible. At any moment, we may get new information or new resources, or we may lose support we thought we had. We must be able to adapt to the new situation instead of getting caught in old routines."

Consensus

"We build a consensus instead of looking to one person to make decisions. We talk through issues and consider everyone's opinion. Then, we decide on a course of action that each team member can buy in to."

Initiative

"We take the initiative to get our goals accomplished. Everyone on this team wants to do a great job. We don't sit back and wait to get moving. I like it because I know we're making positive changes for our company."

Question

Practice what you've learned. Identify the qualities that develop team synergy.

Options:

1. The team has a clear mission.
2. The team has a process for building consensus.

3. Team members openly share information.
4. The team leader makes all the decisions.
5. Team members compete with one another.

Answer:

Actually, team synergy comes from several qualities, including cooperation, open communication, consensus-building, and a clear mission.

Option 1: This answer is correct. One quality that leads to team synergy is the team having a clear mission because when they know what needs to be accomplished it is easy for the team members to stay focused.

Option 2: Correct. If the team has a process for building consensus it will develop synergy. Rather than one person making all the decisions, the team talks through issues and considers everyone's opinion, then decides on a course of action.

Option 3: Correct. When team members openly share information, they build synergy. Each member always knows the important facts, which makes them more committed to the team goal.

Option 4: This answer is incorrect. If the team leader makes all the decisions, there will not be synergy because each team member may not feel committed or tied to the team goal.

Option 5: This answer is incorrect. If team members compete with one another, there will be no synergy because each person is out for himself and not the team.

Team synergy can be a dynamic force that helps groups accomplish major goals. But this effect is only created through a combination of important factors. Without this synergy, it's difficult for teams to succeed.

DEVELOPING TEAM INTELLIGENCE

Developing Team Intelligence

What makes a great team? If a team has problems, should you give up on it? If the workplace changes, should the team change?

Team success is a combination of many factors. Teams can be developed over time. While changes in group members may be necessary, development is also important to success. You'll examine:

- why it's important to have the right people in the right jobs,
- how feedback and support can increase success,
- why encouraging and evaluating contribute to group growth.

Question

Which of the following characteristics contribute to team intelligence?

Options:

1. Group members are selected based on a predetermined set of competencies.

2. Team members avoid giving one another feedback.

3. The team has a process for integrating new skills into the work environment.

4. Group members provide support for one another.

Answer:

Actually, it takes a combination of good job fit, support, and feedback for a team to succeed. The group should also have a process for integrating new learning.

Option 1: Correct. Selection based on a predetermined set of competencies contributes to team intelligence. Companies that match employees and jobs have determined what it takes to do the job well and they hire based on this information.

Option 2: This answer is incorrect. If team members avoided giving one another feedback, no one would know what they were doing well or where there opportunities lied.

Option 3: This answer is correct. Integrating new skills into the work environment is important to team intelligence because it shows flexibility and acceptance of change, which is critical to success.

Option 4: This answer is correct. Providing support for one another contributes to team intelligence because it shows that team members appreciate each other and have confidence in each other's abilities.

In this lesson, you'll explore the best way to build a team. You'll also examine how to develop the team by encouraging growth and learning, and by promoting behavior change when appropriate.

By following the processes in this lesson, you will be able to help develop the team's emotional intelligence.

The ad for a financial company says, "Friendly people wanted for customer service positions." But is this really enough to do a good job in customer service?

Probably not. Studies show that customer service can be one of the most stressful jobs around. Turnover is high; employees burn out quickly. There are people who shine in this position and there's a reason why: They've been matched to the right job. Good hiring is more than guesswork and it contributes to the success of the team. An emotionally intelligent team has the right people doing the right jobs.

Companies that match employees and jobs have determined what it takes to do the job well. They hire people based on these competencies. These employers design training that supports the competencies that are important to success.

Kyle manages the customer service department. He's working with Laura, a consultant, to improve his company's recruiting. Laura is going to walk Kyle through three important steps.

- identifying the competencies representatives need,
- outlining a supportive training program
- developing a process for matching people to jobs.

Laura interviewed Brad, a strong performer, to learn more about what it takes to succeed in customer service.

Laura: Can you describe a typical concern that you encounter--some kind of problem that you have to solve?

Brad: Well, brokers often call because the sales charge has been misapplied to their accounts. They're usually upset because that means they're not being paid correctly.

Laura: How do you handle a situation like that?

Brad: First, you have to calm them down. I apologize for the mistake, then assure them that I'll work with them until the problem's resolved. I don't ask questions or even look at my computer until they're not as angry.

Laura: After they're calm, what approach do you take next?

Brad: I have to do a little detective work. I need to ask several questions to figure out what type of sales charge they qualify for. Then, I need to evaluate how the charges have been applied. Finally, I need to figure out where the error occurred.

Laura: After you figure out the cause of the error, do you have any additional conflicts with them?

Brad: Sometimes the brokers are wrong. If so, it takes some patience to get them to understand their error.

Laura's prepared a list of the skills for success in customer service. She based these on interviews with Brad and other employees, as well as observation. The competencies for an effective customer service representative are:

- a friendly personality,
- conflict management,
- stress management,
- problem-solving
- product knowledge.

Laura recommends that Kyle look for employees who display many of these abilities. But first, she thinks he should consider building a training program that supports the competencies for effective customer service.

See each action for Laura's training recommendations.

Identify competencies

"You've identified the qualities your customer service reps need. They need to be outgoing and able to solve problems and manage stress. They also need to be good listeners and have sufficient knowledge of the products."

Design training

"You may be able to find employees with good quality skills, but you can't expect to hire the perfect employee. You'll need to design a training program that supports these competencies."

Prepare employees

"Product knowledge, stress management, and conflict management skills should be part of new employee training. Use training to prepare employees for day-to-day life on the job."

Improve gaps

"When you find skill gaps, use training as a way to build these skills, but be reasonable. You can't change someone from a hermit into an outgoing person, but you may be able to improve her listening skills with new techniques."

How can Kyle find the right person for each job? He needs to match people to the competencies Laura identified as critical to customer service jobs. He can do much of this during the interview process.

See each action for Laura's advice on matching the right person to the right job.

Look for the competencies

Interview candidates based on the necessary competencies. Ask questions that reveal stress management and problem-solving skills. Look for outgoing people. Ask for information about conflict management experience.

Assess ability to grow

It's also important that the candidates have an ability to grow in the position. Ask questions about mistakes or growth opportunities they have experienced. Their ability to admit mistakes and describe growth experiences will indicate their self-awareness.

Identify training needs

Remember, you may find great candidates who may only need some training to perform. If their product knowledge needs work or they don't have a lot of experience with conflict management, you may be able to fill these gaps with new-employee training.

Evaluate thoroughly

Don't just rely on the candidates' description of themselves. You might want to set up mock customer calls or have them go through a role-play. There are tests that can evaluate problem-solving skills. You can also use references to provide some information.

Question

Lynne hires flight attendants for a major airline. It's important that the flight crew be prepared and capable, or a serious accident could occur. If she wants to make a good match between a candidate and a job opening, what should she do?

Options:

1. She should hire based on common sense about what it takes to be a good flight attendant.

2. Lynne should determine the competencies needed to be a capable flight attendant.

3. Lynne should thoroughly evaluate each candidate based on the competencies.

4. Lynne should implement a training strategy that supports the necessary competencies.

Answer:

Actually, Lynne should determine the competencies for flight attendants and hire based on this information. She should evaluate each candidate in multiple ways, rather than relying on one piece of information.

Option 1: Incorrect. She should not simply hire based on common sense because while it is important for this type of position, if it's the only criteria Lynne uses, she will miss out on a number of key competencies critical for flight attendant success.

Option 2: This answer is correct. In order to make a good match, Lynne should determine the competencies needed to be a capable flight attendant because this will ensure she is looking for the right skills in her potential employees.

Option 3: This choice is correct. Lynne should thoroughly evaluate each candidate based on the competencies in order to find a good match, which will ensure that she has matched the right employee to the position.

Option 4: Correct. Lynne should implement a training strategy that supports the competencies. Since there will be skills specific to the job that new employees don't have, her training program should match the competencies required to perform the job.

Managers like Kyle often struggle with the complex process of building a strong team. To build the foundation for an emotionally intelligent team, he must match the right people to the right jobs. Laura has helped him begin this process by identifying the competencies that are critical to success. Kyle must evaluate job candidates based on these competencies and build a training program that supports the skills for success.

Eric, a paralegal in a law firm, hated performance appraisals. They made him feel like he was being attacked the entire time.

This is how a lot of people feel when they're given feedback at work. Many supervisors and managers save feedback for performance reviews, then treat feedback as a tool to tear employees down instead of build them up. You'll explore:

- why empathy is important during feedback,
- how to build self-confidence through feedback,
- why it's important to be delicate,
- how to provide support for employees who are struggling.

Empathy is an important skill during almost every workplace interaction. It's especially important in feedback situations, in which the provider and the receiver may be tense.

See With empathy and Without empathy for two improvement feedback messages.

With empathy

"I'm concerned about the team's schedule. I know you're busy, but when meetings don't start on time, they end up lasting a long time."

Without empathy

"You're late a lot and it really makes me angry. You obviously don't have respect for your team's schedules."

Wendy manages the branch office of a large bank. She has several employees and knows that in order to develop her team's emotional intelligence, she has to give input into performance on a regular basis.

See each factor for Wendy's comments about feedback.

A Building Tool

"I use feedback to "build" employees. I want them to have the careers they want, and feedback is a tool to get them there. I don't want to constantly criticize or tear them down. I want them to know what they are doing well."

Frequency

"I don't just give feedback during a review--it's an everyday process. We all give feedback to each other--I'm open to hearing information about myself. After all, I can't grow as a manager unless I know what works and what doesn't."

Focus on Positives

"Feedback is not the same as criticism. People need to know what they're good at and they need to hear it often. We all take pride in our skills and I try to reinforce this pride for my employees, rather than tear them down."

Delicacy

"My employees don't have weaknesses; they have opportunities for improvement. It's important to give this information delicately. I don't want to destroy self-confidence by pointing out behavior that needs to change."

Support is an important partner to feedback. People need support when they are trying to grow or change direction in a job. Support can range from providing more positive feedback to referrals to employee assistance programs.

Extra support is often required during certain career milestones.

See each circumstance for more information regarding support needs.

additional responsibility

People often need support when they are promoted or take on new tasks. This is a growth period for employees-- they need to acquire new skills and behaviors. Mentoring and training can often provide the support necessary for this transition.

personal problems

Many people go through difficult times in their personal lives that affect their work. These can include divorce, illness, and financial problems. During these times, an employee assistance program or an outside counselor may provide the necessary support.

interpersonal problems

Sometimes, personal difficulties spring up. People may not work well together or they may have personal issues that cloud the tasks. During these times, coaching and feedback can help change behaviors that lead to conflict situations.

concern about career direction

People often have concerns about their jobs, such as, "Do I like this type of work?" or, "Do I want to be in this position?" In this case, they may need to discuss career goals and opportunities that could enrich their careers. They might want to learn new skills or try new tasks.

Question

Benjamin is working to develop his team's emotional intelligence. He knows that feedback and support are critical to the development process and he wants to model these behaviors effectively. What behaviors should

Benjamin demonstrate when providing feedback and support?

Options:

1. Benjamin should give feedback only about weaknesses.

2. Benjamin should reinforce team members' confidence about what they're doing well.

3. Benjamin should use empathy in the feedback process.

Answer:

Actually, Benjamin should give team members positive, motivating feedback. This will boost their confidence. Empathy is also important to the feedback process.

Option 1: Incorrect. If Benjamin only gave feedback about weaknesses, the work environment would not be very positive and his employees would be unmotivated. Feedback should be positive and weaknesses should be treated as challenges.

Option 2: Correct. When providing feedback and support, Benjamin should reinforce team members' confidence about what they are doing well because they take pride in their skills and reinforcing this pride is important.

Option 3: This answer is correct. Bruce should use empathy in the feedback process because both he and his employee may be tense. Delicacy is the key.

Remember, feedback and support help people improve. As team members develop, their emotional intelligence will increase. The following points are important to remember when providing feedback and support:

- Positive feedback builds confidence.

- It's important to use empathy, especially when giving feedback about areas for improvement.
- Team members often need extra support during career milestones. This can include training, coaching, and mentoring.

Have you ever attended a training class, only to return to the office and put the binder on the shelf? Have you ever learned a skill, then forgotten it because you never used it on the job?

Question

Employers spend millions of dollars every year sending employees through training and development programs. Often, these skills end up forgotten. Why do skills go unused?

Options:

1. Employees aren't rewarded for changed behavior.
2. Workers don't get to use new skills on the job.
3. Employers don't consider the skills important to job success. 4. Employees are too overwhelmed to change their behavior.

Answer:

Actually, these are all some of the many reasons why employees don't change their behavior.

Option 1: This is a correct choice. Employees forget new skills because they are not rewarded for their changed behavior. The employer should provide support and reinforcement during the change process.

Option 2: This answer is correct. Skills end up forgotten when they don't get used on the job. If a new skill is not utilized right away, it usually won't get used at all.

Option 3: This answer is correct. Employees end up forgetting new skills when employers do not consider them important to job success. Often an employee will learn a new skill that their manager does not reinforce on the job.

Option 4: Correct. Skills end up forgotten when employees are too overwhelmed to change their behavior. Because adopting a new skill or behavior adds time initially, in a high paced environment this learning curve may not be allowed.

Everyone learns new skills and techniques. Some learning takes place in the classroom, while other behaviors are learned more informally. Employers frequently request a new process or strategy for doing work or interacting with customers. Why do so many of these initiatives die out? Because they aren't supported on the job and workers aren't given the encouragement they need to put new actions in place.

The change process requires goal-setting, support, and reinforcement. Without these critical factors, things will usually stay the same.

Learning and growth should be encouraged in every environment. However, development plans are most effective when the following factors are considered:

- Change should be self-directed. Each person should seek out growth through his own initiative.
- Development plans should be tailored to the individual, so it incorporates her interests and goals.
- Each person has a different starting point and is going to a different place.

Nancy's boss, Norman, is working on a development plan with her. He wants her to practice better time management. She's working long hours and is exhausted, partly because of a need for more efficiency. However, this is a large goal, and it's hard to measure.

Norman helps Nancy develop a more realistic learning plan.

See each development aspect for Norman's comments about the development plan.

Small Goals

"*Manage your time better* isn't a clear goal. Instead, we set some small goals. The first was that Nancy would leave the office by 5 p.m. three times a week without taking work home with her."

Frequent Success

"Nancy can succeed more frequently with smaller goals. Her next goal is to work on her delegation skills by handing over two tasks each day to one of her employees. That's something she can succeed with."

Provide Support

"This is a big change for Nancy--she'll need support. She's attending a course on time management. I'll act as a mentor. We'll meet once a week to discuss time management techniques and how things are going."

Evaluate

"Nancy's time management skills will be evaluated regularly. She'll be rewarded if her skills improve. She won't be rewarded for working 70-hour weeks when her goal is to delegate and cut back her hours."

Employees are often told to exhibit one behavior but find they're judged on other criteria. When behaviors aren't part of the evaluation process, change won't occur.

See each goal for two examples of employees who were encouraged to improve their customer service skills.

Customer interactions

"They say they want more quality. But our customer interactions are timed and that's what we're rated on. It doesn't make sense."

Customer satisfaction

"Our primary goal is to satisfy the customer. Sometimes that takes a time investment. We're judged on the quality of the interaction, not the length."

It's important to encourage and evaluate the behaviors that employees are learning. New behaviors should become part of the performance evaluation process. But, before employees are rated, they should have other support systems in place.

See each action to learn how to support integrating new skills and techniques into working life.

Value the right behavior

Make sure the behaviors you ask for are the ones you value. If you say you want good customer service--reward it. It's easy to set conflicting goals like quality service and speedy customer interactions. This confuses employees, and they'll pick the behavior that's rewarded.

Encourage employees

Encourage people to try new behaviors. Give them opportunities to practice in a non- threatening environment. If workers have to use a new machine to produce products, let them practice without time or quality expectations at first.

Provide support

Support for new skills is especially important. Mentoring, buddy systems, and teams can reduce the stress involved in learning. It also helps to approach learning as a team. Some groups have weekly meetings to discuss how to put learning in place.

Establish measurements

Find ways to measure learning. Set small goals, such as, "During week two, let's move to a three-day timeline for processing the loans we've learned about." Celebrate the success, then move to a new goal. "During week four, we'll try for a two-and-a-half day timeline."

Provide feedback.

Feedback is critical to the change process. Employees should receive positive and growth-oriented feedback about how they're implementing new skills. They should receive suggestions and constructive criticism so the new skill is implemented effectively.

Question

Martin is a team leader who is working on improving his team's emotional intelligence. What actions can Martin take to encourage and evaluate his employees?

Options:

1. He should ask his employees to set only long-term, big-picture goals.

2. He should give his workers a chance to practice new skills.

3. He should ensure that he is rewarding the behaviors he's asked employees to use.

4. He should ask employees to avoid using new, unfamiliar skills.

Answer:

Actually, Martin should encourage his employees to practice the skills they're working to improve. He should also make sure he's rewarding the behaviors he approves of.

Option 1: This answer is incorrect. To encourage and evaluate his employees, Martin should not ask his employees to set only long-term, big-picture goals. Because long-term goals can be intimidating, they may not be obtainable.

Option 2: Correct. In order to encourage his employees to use the new skills they learned, Martin should give them a chance to practice before using the skill on the job. This should reduce the stress involved in learning and performing a new behavior.

Option 3: This answer is correct. Martin can encourage his employees by rewarding the behaviors he has asked employees to use because this will reinforce their use and value.

Option 4: This answer is incorrect. Martin should not ask his employees to avoid using new, unfamiliar skills because they will never grow or change.

It can be difficult to change behaviors. However, this learning process is an important key to emotional intelligence. If employees receive the proper support while they're trying to integrate new behaviors into their work days, they're more likely to be successful.

As employees improve, they increase the team's knowledge, abilities and, most important, the team's ability to grow and adapt.

The glue that holds today's work teams together is made up of social competence, the ability to influence others, participation, and collaboration. Teams also need an ability to develop and grow over time. They need to be flexible and adapt to change. People and teams alike have the ability to develop their emotional intelligence--an important factor in their success.

CHAPTER IV - INCREASING EMOTIONAL INTELLIGENCE

CHAPTER IV - Increasing Emotional Intelligence

How can you increase your "people smarts"? First, you'll need a strong understanding of emotional intelligence. Then, you will need to understand how and what you need to improve.

In this chapter, you'll examine:
- how emotional and intellectual intelligence differ,
- why emotional intelligence matters at work,
- where emotional intelligence comes from,
- how to improve your emotional intelligence.

EMOTIONAL AND INTELLECTUAL INTELLIGENCE

Emotional and Intellectual Intelligence
Do you ever wonder why your mind works the way it does? Are you ever curious about what "smart" really means?

The brain has evolved since the beginning of human history. In recent years, research has focused on the importance of emotional intelligence to workplace and relationship success. In this lesson, you'll explore:
- two types of intelligence: emotional and intellectual,
- the difference between constructive and destructive thinking,
- how rational and experiential minds work.

See each point for more information about how emotional intelligence is important to your success.

Managing conflict
Conflict is a part of nearly every work environment. As you build your emotional intelligence, you'll increase your conflict management abilities. You'll learn tools to deal

with others in tense situations. As your skills improve, you'll be able to manage conflict effectively.

Thinking constructively

The way you think affects how you feel and behave. You'll improve your thought processes and learn to think in constructive ways. As you increase your emotional intelligence, you'll learn to think in ways that help rather than hurt you.

Forming relationships

Your effectiveness at forming and building relationships with others relates directly to your emotional intelligence. You'll learn to improve your relationships with management, customers, and co-workers. You'll form strong alliances in the workplace.

Question

Why is emotional intelligence important to your success in life?

Options:

1. You'll have the ability to avoid conflict situations.
2. You'll think in ways that help rather than hurt you.
3. You'll ensure that your career is rewarding.
4. You'll form strong alliances at work.

Answer:

Actually, emotional intelligence and the way you think affect your life success dramatically. Emotional intelligence relates to your ability to form strong relationships with others.

Option 1: This answer is incorrect. Emotional intelligence will not give you the ability to avoid conflict situations but when you are in conflict, emotional intelligence will help you manage it effectively.

Option 2: This answer is correct. Emotional intelligence is important to your success in life because it can help you think in ways that help rather than hurt you. You will improve your thought processes and learn to think in constructive ways.

Option 3: Incorrect. Ensuring that you will have a rewarding career is not directly related to emotional intelligence. Rather emotional intelligence relates to your ability to manage conflict, think constructively, and form strong relationships with others.

Option 4: This answer is correct. Emotional intelligence will help you form strong alliances at work because you'll learn to improve your relationships with management, customers, and co-workers.

In this lesson, you'll build an understanding of emotional and intellectual intelligence and how each works. You'll see how your emotional intelligence affects your capacity for success. This understanding will lead you to value the importance of emotional intelligence.

You'll also explore how the mind works and two important brain functions: the rational mind and the experiential mind.

Can someone be smart in more than one way? Are some people intelligent but lacking in common sense?

There is more than one way to be smart. A person can be strong in either type of intelligence. Some people are competent in both types of intelligence. You'll explore:

- the two types of intelligence,
- the function of intellect,
- the characteristics of emotional intelligence.

Emotional intelligence and intellect must both be considered when viewing intelligence. Intellect is the traditional way to view brainpower. However, as the world becomes more complex, emotional intelligence becomes more important.

See each characteristic for more information about intellectual and emotional intelligence.

Problem-solving

Intellect refers to your problem-solving abilities, including your ability to reason and process information.

Feelings

Emotional intelligence is your ability to understand and deal effectively with feelings. This includes understanding other people's emotions.

Intellect is one important component of intelligence. It plays a specific role in life. However, intellect alone doesn't explain behavior. "Smart" people do stupid things. People with average or low intelligence can have happy, fulfilling lives. It's important to understand how intellect plays into intelligence and the limits of the rational mind.

Review each question for more information about intellect.

How does it work?

Intellect is the conscious, problem-solving part of your mind. When you're aware of your thoughts, you are using intellect. You use it to make decisions like, "The car behind me is too close. I'm moving into the slow lane so the driver can pass me."

What does it do?

Your intellect is your ability to solve problems. You use intellect to reason through a problem. You also depend on intellect to process information. Your intellect determines the speed of the car behind you and checks the slow lane to make sure it's clear before you move over.

Why is it important?

Intellect is the rational part of your mind. It's based on logic and is not tied to emotions. Intellect helps you make decisions and determine the best action when you're not emotional. This type of intelligence helps you succeed in information-processing environments, like school.

What are its limitations?

Your intellect can be slow. In some situations, you won't have time to process information and decide on action based on the facts. Intellect is measured by IQ, which describes how "smart" you are. However, IQ alone doesn't predict how successful you will be.

Emotional intelligence is the second type of brainpower that contributes to intelligence. This type of thinking works with intellect to determine behavior. Emotional intelligence is a more reliable predictor of success than intellect. People with high IQs don't always build satisfying lives. Those with strong emotional intelligence navigate relationships more effectively, and are more likely to be successful in their personal and professional lives.

See each question to learn more about emotional intelligence.

What is it?

Emotional intelligence is the ability to understand your feelings and the emotional states of those around you. It's your ability to comprehend these emotions and to manage them effectively.

Where does it come from?

Your emotional intelligence comes from your experiences. Each interaction and event in your life leaves an imprint. This information is stored and retrieved to help you make instant emotional evaluations and decisions.

How does it work?

Emotional intelligence happens below the surface. It's pre-conscious--it happens before you use your intellect. You aren't always aware of the navigations of your emotional mind. You're only aware of your impressions and instincts.

Why is it important?

Emotional intelligence is often referred to as common sense. This brainpower helps you get along with others and build strong relationships. It helps you say the right thing and accurately judge how the other person is reacting.

Question

What is the value of understanding emotional intelligence and intellect? Complete this sentence:

Emotional intelligence and intellect:

Options:

1. stay fixed throughout your life.
2. can increase and decrease.

Answer:

Actually, you can increase both your intellect and emotional intelligence. They both fluctuate based on experience, environment, and education.

Option 1: This answer is incorrect. Emotional intelligence and intellect do not stay fixed throughout your life because if it did, you would never learn from your experiences or additional education.

Option 2: This choice is correct. Emotional intelligence and intellect can increase and decrease because through experiences and education, we can increase our knowledge and emotional sense.

Intellect is based on your capacity to solve problems. By increasing your education, whether formally or outside an academic environment, you can increase how much you know.

Emotional intelligence is based on how constructively you use your emotions. By learning from experiences, you can increase your emotional "sense."

Question

Practice what you've learned. Choose the characteristics of emotional and intellectual intelligence.

Options:

1. Your IQ determines your level of emotional intelligence.
2. IQ includes the ability to solve problems.
3. IQ always remains stable.
4. Behavior is determined by emotional intelligence and IQ.

Answer:

Actually, emotional intelligence and IQ are separate abilities, but both play into behavior. Both can change over time.

Option 1: This answer is incorrect. Your IQ does not determine your level of emotional intelligence, it determines your level of intellect.

Option 2: Correct. One characteristic of intellectual intelligence is your ability to solve problems because it's based on logic and is not tied to emotions. Intellect helps you make decisions and determine the best action when you're not emotional.

Option 3: This answer is incorrect. IQ does not always remain stable because by increasing your education, whether formally or outside an academic environment, you can increase how much you know.

Option 4: This answer is correct. Emotional intelligence and IQ, or the ability to reason and feel, work together to determine behavior.

Emotional intelligence and intellect both contribute to your intelligence. Intellect is often associated with academic success. It relates to logic and problem-solving abilities.

Your ability to deal with people comes from your emotional intelligence. Both types of intelligence can increase or decrease, depending on your environment.

Cora and Justin are both copy editors for a magazine. They face tight deadlines and enormous pressure from their boss, Frank.

Justin thrives in this environment; however, Cora seems worn down by the constant stress. What makes Justin and Cora react so differently?

The difference is constructive thinking. Justin's mind works in a way that helps him thrive, while Cora's thought process adds to her difficulties. In this topic, you'll explore:
- the definition of constructive thinking,
- characteristics of destructive thinkers,
- characteristics of constructive thinkers.

Cora and Justin represent two kinds of thinking. Justin is a constructive thinker. This kind of thinking helps him to be successful. Cora's thought process is destructive, which inhibits her progress.

See each type for more information about constructive and destructive thinking.

Constructive Thinking

Justin thinks in a way that helps him solve problems, with a minimum amount of stress. His thoughts are positive and action-oriented.

Destructive Thinking

Cora gets caught up in and distracted by stress and deadlines. She thinks in a negative way, which prevents her from moving forward.

Cora's destructive thinking shows up in several behaviors. Her boss, Frank, has noticed some of the thought processes that stall Cora's progress.

Review each example of Cora's destructive thinking and then select each of Frank's corresponding comments to find out what he feels about her worries.

Negative Thinking

"I just know something is going to throw me off track once I start making progress. It's always something--a computer crash, a last-minute change, or a new project. I can't do things right under this kind of pressure."

Frank's Comments

"Cora looks at her environment negatively. She only sees the downside. She expects the worst to happen. With that kind of attitude, things often go wrong. If she looked at things in a positive, proactive way, she'd have fewer problems."

Inflexibility

"Frank asks me to switch around deadlines all the time. How can he expect me to finish anything with such chaotic planning? I need to work on one thing at a time or I can't do my work properly."

Frank's Comments

"Cora doesn't think flexibly. She expects the world to be predictable, which it isn't. Changing deadlines is a reality of the publishing business. It throws Cora into complete upheaval. If she were flexible, she probably wouldn't feel as pressured."

Overly Sensitive

"Frank is always finding problems with my work. He's out to get me. He doesn't support me enough. I feel like I'm being attacked all the time. My projects come back with corrections all over them."

Frank's Comments

"Cora is overly sensitive to criticism. My job is to edit her work, which means I'm inevitably going to make changes. It's the nature of the job--I do the same to all the staff members' work. Cora chooses to take it personally."

Not Learning

"I run into a problem with research all the time. Frank never thinks I have enough sources. I always have to go back and find more information. It really eats up my time to do this re-work."

Frank's Comments

"Cora doesn't learn from experience. I've sent her back repeatedly to do a more thorough background check on stories. She should be doing this work up front instead of running into the same problem again and again."

Justin takes a constructive thinking approach, which helps him succeed in his work environment. His

thought process tends to be more toward positive and problem-solving ideas, rather than the stress- inducing thinking that Cora uses. Frank notices the difference Justin's constructive thinking makes.

See each positive approach to learn what Frank thinks.

Acceptance

"Justin knows what he can change and accepts what can't be changed. Multiple priorities are and always will be a reality of the publishing business. However, Justin did ask to change our staffing process because it was delaying our schedules."

Self-confidence

"Justin has an appropriate level of self-confidence. He knows what he's good at and where he needs work. He values himself and isn't overly self-critical. This confidence helps him tackle challenging projects because he believes he has the ability to succeed."

Avoiding labeling

"I notice employees get into the habit of labeling others all the time. They think one editor is 'bad' or another is 'good.' They judge people as being for or against them. Justin doesn't fall into this trap. He sees that people bring a variety of skills and approaches to the table and he appreciates everyone."

Flexibility

"Justin is flexible. He can adapt to change without becoming unduly stressed. This makes his life easier, especially since stress is constant in our environment. He can also see things from more than one point of view, which helps him adapt to others."

Problem-solving focus

"Justin is focused on solving problems and moving forward. This is better than complaining or trying to avoid challenging situations. It's an action-focused approach that helps him be positive. Once he's made headway toward solving a problem, it becomes less of a stress factor."

Question

Barbara recently got into an argument with her new officemate, Trent. He was working hard to meet a deadline. She was on the phone, planning a social event for the evening. Trent started yelling at her and calling her lazy. How can Barbara think constructively about this event?

Options:

1. She should talk with Trent about the problem when he's calm.

2. Trent will be difficult to share an office with.

3. She should be conscious of Trent's moods before she uses the phone.

4. She should realize that she was wrong for making a personal call when she shares an office.

Answer:

Actually, Barbara should focus on positive actions rather than blaming Trent or herself. She should be conscious of how she contributed to the problem without being too hard on herself.

Option 1: Correct. By thinking constructively about this event, Barbara decides she should talk with Trent about the problem when he's calm because in order to solve the problem, they should both focus on the positive aspects of the situation.

Option 2: This answer is incorrect. Barbara is thinking destructively in determining it will be difficult to share an office with Trent. She is looking at her environment in a negative light and not thinking constructively about this event.

Option 3: This answer is correct. By thinking constructively about this event, Barbara decides she should be conscious of Trent's moods before she uses the phone. By being flexible, she is able to adapt to others needs.

Option 4: This answer is incorrect. Barbara was thinking destructively when she determined she was wrong for making a personal call. She was being overly sensitive when she took Trent's comments personally.

Constructive thinking is an important aspect of emotional intelligence. Your thought process can strongly contribute to your success. Destructive thinkers experience a lot of stress and run into multiple problems.

By focusing on positive, problem-solving thoughts instead of negative approaches, you'll be more productive and less tense.

Beth, an advertising executive, was angry with her children before work one morning. She ended up yelling at both of them.

When she got to the office later that morning, Beth found out she'd lost a major client. Now, no matter how frustrated she gets, she doesn't yell at her children before work.

Did Beth lose the client because she yelled at her children? Of course not; the two events are unrelated.

But because one happened before the other, Beth's mind has determined that there was a cause-and-effect relationship. How many times have you engaged in similar mental games, like wearing a special pair of socks for important meetings or taking the same route home from work every day because you've never seen a wreck on that road?

Everyone plays mental games. Where do they come from? They come from our minds, which operate in two ways. There is an experiential mind and a rational mind. Each works in very different ways.

Human brains have developed in many complex ways through the process of evolution. Mental games are just one way the brain learns to cope with its environment. In this topic, you'll explore:
- how the rational mind works,
- why the experiential mind exists,
- how the experiential mind can make mistakes.

The experiential and rational minds both play important roles in the thought and action processes. Each part of the mind uses different types of input to think and make decisions.

See each part of the mind for more information.

Rational mind

The rational mind uses logic and evidence to process information and make decisions. This is the conscious part of your mind.

Experiential mind

The experiential mind is unconscious. It develops based on experience rather than from concrete evidence.

When you are aware that you're thinking, you're using your rational mind. This is the conscious part of the brain you use to plan, analyze, and consider. The rational mind is what people traditionally consider the "brain."

See each area to learn more about the rational mind.

Decision-making

The rational mind uses evidence and facts to make decisions. It wants logical proof and evidence. This is the part of your mind that often evaluates purchasing decisions. You use schedules, prices, and features lists to decide on the best choice.

Emotion
The rational mind is free from emotion. It behaves based on logic and reasoning only. This part of the mind operates especially well during low-emotion events.

Thinking
The rational mind thinks slowly. It plans, analyzes, and considers before deciding on a course of action. When you plan a project, you rely heavily on your rational mind.

Cause and Effect
The rational mind carefully looks for cause-and-effect events. It doesn't jump to conclusions about events--the rational mind would not associate bad news with the person who delivered it.

The experiential mind has developed over thousands of years. It links us closely to other animals, whose minds operate primarily in this way. Its goal is to help you take in information, interpret events, and take instant action. It relies on information you've collected during past experiences to make these decisions.

See each aspect to learn more about the experiential mind.

Learns from experience
The experiential mind uses experiences to make decisions. It learns from each experience, then applies this information to new events. Emotionally significant (good or bad) events help the mind learn and develop.

Reacts quickly
This part of the mind is tied closely to evolution--it's like a survival system. The experiential mind is designed to think fast. This is why you react before you think in some

stressful situations. It's like your reactions "sneak up" on you.

Reacts automatically

The experiential mind isn't conscious. It reacts without conscious thought. If someone tells you of a death in your family, you immediately start to cry. You don't think, "I'm upset; I'm going to cry." Instead, tears start flowing before thoughts are active.

Pays attention to outcome

The experiential mind looks for causes of pleasurable events. It also looks for people or actions to blame when outcomes are not pleasurable. It does this through association, not logical analysis.

Is tied to emotions

The experiential mind seeks to manage your emotions. The goal is to maximize pleasure and minimize pain. It is also more susceptible to emotions. The more happy or upset you become, the more your experiential mind takes over. This is why people can become irrational during times of stress.

The experiential mind makes mistakes because it only looks at outcomes. Imagine that you do a favor for a co-worker one afternoon. Later that day, you win the lottery. The experiential mind may associate the action of doing a favor with the pleasurable outcome of winning the lottery. Likewise, you could hurt a co-worker's feelings, then experience a major computer error the same day. There isn't a cause-and-effect relationship, but the experiential mind has jumped to conclusions.

The experiential mind acts fast. It doesn't have time to use logic. It's the same way wild animals think-- they associate events with outcomes, sometimes in error.

Question
Practice what you've learned. Match the descriptions to one or more of the appropriate characteristics of the rational and experiential minds.
Options:
A. the rational mind
B. the experiential mind
Targets:
1. learns from experience
2. processes information quickly
3. associates outcomes with cause-effect relationships
4. is most active in low-stress situations
Answer:
Actually, the rational mind is active in low-stress situations. The rational mind uses logic, while the experiential mind relies on experience and rapidly processed information.

The experiential mind learns from each experience, then applies this information to new events. Emotionally significant events help the mind learn and develop.

The experiential mind processes information quickly because this part of the mind is tied closely to evolution--it is like a survival system. This is why you react before you think in some stressful situations.

The rational mind associates outcomes with cause-effect relationships. It does not jump to conclusions about events because it looks for associations among events.

The rational mind is most active in low-stress situations. Because the rational mind is free from emotion, it makes slow, in-depth decisions based on logic and reasoning.

The rational and experiential minds are both important parts of the brain. The rational mind makes slow, in-depth decisions using logic and evidence. However, you won't always have time for this kind of analysis.

The experiential mind takes over when quick decisions must be made. It's designed to adapt and respond quickly.

USING EMOTIONAL INTELLIGENCE AT WORK

Using Emotional Intelligence at Work

Can the people around you read your mind? Do they know what you're thinking?

Other people can't read your mind, but they often know what you're thinking by the way you behave. Your thought process directly affects the way you act. In this lesson, you'll examine:
- how high achievers think,
- how you can apply constructive thinking at work,
- why your emotional intelligence affects your well-being.

Constructive thinking is an important part of emotional intelligence. The more positive and action- oriented your thoughts are, the more manageable your emotions will become. By evaluating how you think and identifying the thought processes you can improve, you'll build a road map for becoming a more effective thinker.

Steve, the CEO of a large bank, told Erin, the training department manager, that she'd have to limit costs by 20 percent over the next year.

He expected her to fly off the handle and have a very stressful reaction. Instead, she looked at it as an interesting challenge. She actually managed to improve the training while cutting costs. Steve was very pleasantly surprised.

Erin is a high achiever. Her approach to work and problem-solving helps her achieve more success. She also experiences less frustration along the way than many of her co-workers. In this topic, you'll explore:
- what the characteristics of high achievers are,
- how high achievers approach problems,
- why high achievers experience less stress.

A common trait of high achievers is action orientation. Some people are overwhelmed by problems, mistakes, and conflicts in the workplace. High achievers are able to keep moving.

See each characteristic for information on how Erin's action orientation helps her be a high achiever.

Looks for solutions

Erin looks at a problem and figures out how to solve it. She immediately moves toward action. She doesn't let issues hang over her head.

Overcomes mistakes

Erin doesn't act defeated when she makes a mistake. Instead, she looks for a correction and moves forward as soon as possible.

Erin's action orientation is a very important part of her success. There are other subtle ways that she thinks help her perform effectively. Her boss, Steve, sees Erin behave in ways that help her move forward.

See each characteristic of action orientation for Steve's comments about Erin as a high achiever.

Confident

"Erin has confidence in her decisions. She doesn't worry about making everyone happy, which is impossible. Instead, she tries to make the best decision. She doesn't overreact or take it personally when others disagree."

Flexible

"Erin is a flexible thinker. She's open to compromise with others. She's able to see things from other people's viewpoints instead of being rigid or judgmental. This helps her get along well with her co-workers."

Positive

"Erin doesn't dwell on things that go wrong. She also doesn't worry a lot about things she can't control. She does her best to deal with what's in front of her, which is the best use of her energy."

Realistic

"Erin is an optimist, but she's also realistic. She looks for the best in people whenever possible. Some optimists try to 'fly by the seat of their pants.' Erin hopes for the best but prepares for the worst."

Question

So what difference does the high-achieving mentality make in day-to-day life? Choose the results you think high achievers realize in their lives.

Options:

1. They miss work less frequently.
2. They experience fewer illnesses.
3. They take criticism in stride.
4. They experience less stress in their personal lives.
5. They have rewarding personal relationships.

Answer:

Actually, high achievers feel better, deal with problems more effectively, and have more fulfilling relationships than people who let stress get the better of them.

Option 1: This answer is correct. High achievers miss work less frequently because they experience less stress, which means they are more motivated and are ill less often.

Option 2: This answer is correct. High achievers experience fewer illnesses because they are less stressed, which means they are healthier and happier individuals.

Option 3: This answer is correct. High achievers take criticism in stride. Because they have confidence in their decisions, they don't overreact or take it personally when others disagree.

Option 4: This answer is correct. High achievers experience less stress in their personal lives because they take situations in stride and make the best of the situations they face.

Option 5: This answer is correct. High achievers have rewarding personal relationships because they are able to see things from other people's viewpoints instead of being rigid or judgmental.

Stress is in the eye of the beholder. How you think about the situations you face ultimately determines your reaction. If you look at problems as interesting challenges, you'll react more like Erin. You'll be motivated and inspired instead of frustrated and worn down. Studies show that people who feel less stressed-out think optimistically and make the best of the situations they face.

Studies also show that companies that encourage a positive environment have happier, healthier workers. Positive thinking can make a big difference in productivity and illness rates.

Question

Identify the characteristics of how high achievers think.

Options:

1. High achievers are generally optimistic, but are also realistic.
2. High achievers worry about things they can't control.
3. High achievers correct mistakes quickly.
4. High achievers hold grudges.

Answer:

Actually, high achievers tend to be realistic and optimistic. They tend to be action-oriented, so they don't dwell on mistakes or problems in the past.

Option 1: This is a correct choice. One characteristic of high achievers is they are generally optimistic, but are also realistic. They look for the best in people whenever possible; they hope for the best but prepare for the worst.

Option 2: This answer is incorrect. High achievers do not worry about things they can't control because that would be a waste of energy.

Option 3: This answer is correct. A characteristic of high achievers is that they correct mistakes quickly. Because they don't dwell on things that go wrong, they are able to respond quickly to issues.

Option 4: This answer is incorrect. Holding a grudge is not a characteristic of high achievers because that would be dwelling on the problems of the past and not looking ahead to the future.

High achievers are action-oriented. Instead of wallowing in problems, they move quickly toward solutions. They don't worry about the things they can't control, and they can handle disapproval without losing their self-esteem.

Remember, stress is in the eye of the beholder. You can let events overwhelm you or you can look at problems as interesting challenges.

Tony, a computer analyst at a large food processing company, tries to be a positive thinker most of the time. But how does he stay upbeat in the midst of stress at work?

Tony is experiencing a common problem. While you're developing your constructive thinking skills, you may face challenges at work. In this topic, you'll examine:

- how to maintain a problem-solving focus,
- why being a flexible thinker is important,
- how you can apply constructive thinking on the job.

Derek is a manager of an auto supply chain store. He knows that his employees can face a lot of stress during the workday from both customers and co-workers. He is a believer in the power of constructive thinking. His workers who display this kind of positive, action-oriented thinking are dramatically more effective and much less tense.

See each tip for Derek's advice on constructive thinking.

Be a problem-solver.

"Always focus on solving problems. Try to keep a positive attitude about the challenges you face. Once you identify problem-solving steps and start moving forward, you'll realize that the challenges start becoming less overwhelming and you'll be more productive."

Don't get distracted.

"Every job has distractions. Don't let side issues like office gossip and politics distract you. They will only frustrate you and hinder your performance. You shouldn't worry about your image or what other people think--focus on your tasks and everything else will fall into place."

Be flexible.

"If your behavior isn't working, change it. It's always best to be flexible. If you can't get along with a customer, change your style a little. If it's taking too long to finish a task, try changing the way you do it. Adapt to the situation instead of trying to make the situation fit. It will make your life easier."

Bring out the best in others.

"Try to form relationships that bring out the best in your co-workers and customers. When you encounter a problem, focus on solving the issue rather than demeaning the other person. Build people up; don't tear them down. If you respect other people, they'll become allies."

Derek strongly encourages his employees to be flexible thinkers. When workers can't see someone else's point of view, or take the attitude that, "There's only one right way to do things," relationships with co-workers and customers break down.

Flexible thinking helps people adapt to a wide variety of situations. People with rigid thinking only find success in a limited array of interactions.

Derek knows he must support constructive thinking at work. He's going to talk with Kelly, an experienced manager, about his role in building positive attitudes.

Derek asked Kelly about management's role in constructive thinking.

Kelly: Well, first I recommend looking at illness and absenteeism rates at work.

Derek: If the rates are high, what does that tell you?

Kelly: There are problems in the work environment. When the workplace doesn't encourage constructive thinking, people tend to get sick and miss work more frequently.

Derek: What else can I do to encourage better attitudes?

Kelly: It's important that you clearly communicate performance expectations

Derek: I know performance information is important, but I don't see the connection to constructive thinking.

Kelly: Workers can't take a positive, proactive approach to work without knowing what their targets are. When they know goals, they can get started in the right direction.

Question

Warren manages a group of customer service representatives. He's encouraging his team to implement more constructive thinking. How can Warren think constructively and encourage his team to do the same?

Options:

1. Warren should monitor the team's absenteeism rate to look for signs of stress and fatigue.

2. Warren should focus on his image.

3. When Warren addresses problems, he should avoid demeaning his staff.

4. Warren should communicate clearly about performance expectations.

Answer:
Actually, Warren should be on the lookout for signs of stress and fatigue. He should keep a positive, problem-solving attitude and work to bring out the best in others.

Option 1: Correct. Warren should monitor the team's absenteeism rate to look for signs of stress and fatigue because when the workplace doesn't encourage constructive thinking, people tend to get sick and miss work more frequently.

Option 2: This answer is incorrect. Focusing on his image will not help Warren think more constructively nor will it encourage his team to do the same because his focus will be on himself rather than his team.

Option 3: Correct. Warren will show he is a constructive thinker by addressing problems with his staff in a nondemeaning manner. When he encounters a problem, he should focus on solving the issue rather than demeaning the other person.

Option 4: This answer is correct. Warren can encourage his team by communicating clearly about performance expectations. His staff can then take a positive, proactive approach to work because they will know what their targets are.

It can be a challenge to apply constructive thinking on the job. You'll have to avoid being distracted by side issues such as office gossip or your image, and focus on the task.

Constructive thinking is a positive, action-oriented approach. You'll find that this approach helps you move forward instead of fall behind.

On January 26, the following things all happened to Dave: He was assigned to a new project, a new computer system was installed at his desk, and his sister called to invite him to dinner.

Did Dave have a good day or a bad day?

Dave's day is a matter of interpretation. It could be a good or bad experience depending on Dave's viewpoint. Here's his evaluation of January 26:

- "They're putting me on a lousy project they think is going to fail."
- "The new computer is a big change. I was happy with my old system."
- "My sister probably just wants to borrow money."

Dave's attitude isn't constructive--it's destructive. He's looking at things in the worst possible light, and he assumes that other people have negative motives. His sister was actually inviting him to dinner to celebrate her promotion. The new project presents some career-enriching opportunities, and he received a top-of-the-line computer system. Dave's negative emotions have the potential to damage his career and his relationships with others.

In this topic, you'll explore how underlying thought processes produce emotions. You'll examine typical reactions, and learn about the first step in changing your emotions.

Your emotions aren't actually caused by events. Imagine that you're upset with your manager, Susan, because she gave you a mediocre performance review. Your initial explanation might be, "Susan made me mad." But Susan herself didn't actually cause your anger. The process is much more complicated.

See each stage for information on how emotions are produced.

The event takes place
First, the event has to occur. Susan gives you your performance review and you receive a lower rating than you'd been hoping for.
You interpret the event
You interpret the event: "This is not the performance rating I was hoping for. This is a lower rating than I wanted." At this point, you haven't yet had an emotional reaction; you're making a logical assessment of the facts.
You decide how you should react
Based on your interpretation, "This performance rating is too low," you will now decide on the appropriate reaction, which could range from fear to anger. Subconsciously, you decide that anger is the appropriate emotion for this event.
The emotion is produced
You now produce the emotion of anger and begin to feel the symptoms. The entire process takes place quickly and subconsciously. Susan didn't make you angry--you've interpreted the event and decided the appropriate emotional reaction is anger.

Every emotion plays a role. Each of these mental states exists for a reason and brings benefits and disadvantages. The four main emotions are anger, fear, sadness, and happiness.

See the benefits and problems associated with each of these emotional reactions.
Benefits of Sadness
Sadness helps you step back from a situation and find a way to cope. It provides mourning time and an opportunity to reflect. When you're sad, you're more likely

to re-evaluate your actions and priorities and think about the changes you need to make.

Problems with Sadness

When you're sad, you can become paralyzed. You can feel so bad that you're unable to take action and change bad situations. Sadness can affect you physically and increase the likelihood of illness.

Benefits of Anger

Anger comes from the feeling that someone is wrong or bad and should be punished. Anger helps you "attack." It protects your self-esteem. It reinforces your beliefs and helps motivate you toward decisions.

Problems with Anger

Your anger alienates you from others. It is physically stressful. It makes you prejudiced and blind to your own faults. Anger serves a purpose, but can be very destructive to your relationships.

Benefits of Happiness

Happiness is a good feeling. It makes you want to get involved with others. You're ready to try new things and explore challenges. Others want to be around you when you're happy.

Problems with Happiness

When you are happy, you're much less cautious. You may not plan or take appropriate precautions. Often, when you're happy, you feel like you can conquer the world. This can lead to unrealistic expectations, which ultimately lead to disappointment.

Benefits of Fear

Fear produces the "fight or flight" urge. It can be very motivating. It makes you aware of the threats you face and helps you prepare yourself and take precautions. Fear is instigated by uncertainty.

Problems with Fear

Fear can generate a great deal of tension. It's difficult to concentrate and be creative when you're afraid. It creates stress. Fear is a problem when it's unrealistic. It prevents you from concentrating on important issues.

The first step you can take toward changing your emotional reactions is recognizing how you react. By understanding your reaction, you'll begin to distinguish between the event and your emotions. You'll realize that other people don't cause your feelings. The reaction comes from the underlying thought process.

Becky talked to Mark about a recent time when she was angry.

Mark: What was the event that made you angry?

Becky: Terry deleted files off my computer when he used it the other day. I was angry. I felt that Terry didn't respect my property and that he deleted files because he didn't feel that my work was important.

Mark: When you thought about that, did you see any flaws in your logic?

Becky: Sure. My thought process was based on the idea that Terry intentionally deleted files, which may not necessarily be true. The whole thing may have been an accident.

Becky has made the first step toward regulating her emotions. She's identified the thought process that led her to anger. Now that she's aware of her thinking habits, she can identify why her emotion might not be appropriate. In this case, she's realized that she assumed Terry had a negative intention, when the situation might have been an accident.

Question

Craig was supposed to meet with Karen at 10:30 to discuss project specifications. At 11:15, Karen still hadn't shown up. How does Craig's thought process produce emotion?

Options:

1. Craig interprets the event to mean that Karen thinks his time isn't valuable.

2. Craig feels the emotion of irritation.

3. Craig feels irritation because he thinks Karen doesn't value his time.

4. Craig logically and consciously decides to be irritated.

Answer:

Actually, the event happens and Craig makes his interpretation. He will then select and feel an emotion based on his interpretation of the event.

Option 1: This answer is correct. When Craig interprets the event to mean that Karen thinks his time is not valuable, he has not yet had an emotional reaction; he is making a logical assessment of the facts.

Option 2: This answer is correct. Based on his interpretation of Karen's lateness, Craig decides on the appropriate reaction, which in this case is the emotion of irritation.

Option 3: This is a correct choice. Craig's thought process produces irritation because he thinks Karen doesn't value his time. Karen didn't produce the irritation, Craig interpreted the event and decided on the appropriate emotional reaction.

Option 4: This answer is incorrect. The emotional reaction Craig has is not based on a logical and conscious decision because there is an event associated to his reaction.

There are several emotions you can experience: happiness, anger, fear, and sadness are four of them. These feelings aren't directly caused by events. You go through a thought process that interprets events and identifies a corresponding reaction.

Your understanding of this thought process is the first step toward changing your emotional behavior.

THE SOURCE OF EMOTIONAL INTELLIGENCE

The Source of Emotional Intelligence
Emotional intelligence is widely recognized as a key to success in business and personal relationships. Where does this brainpower come from?

Emotional intelligence is complicated. It is a combination of confidence, self-image, attitude, and learning from experiences. In this lesson, you'll explore:
- why people form beliefs,
- how constructive thinking develops over time,
- why life experiences affect constructive thinking.

In this lesson, you'll have the opportunity to learn where emotional intelligence comes from. Why is this knowledge valuable?

See each benefit to learn more about why it's important to learn about the source of emotional intelligence.

Improving relationships
If you understand why you act the way you do, you'll be able to manage your behavior better. When you improve the way you act, your relationships with other people will

improve. You'll be less likely to get into unproductive conflict and damage important alliances.

Understanding thought processes

When you learn more about where emotional intelligence comes from, you'll learn how your mind works. You'll examine your thought processes, which is the first step toward improving the way you think.

Exploring emotions

Emotions are caused by belief systems. When you learn more about how your feelings are created, you'll understand why you experience emotions. You'll also learn to manage these feelings because you will understand the source of your emotions.

Question

Can emotional intelligence grow and develop over time? Complete this sentence:

Emotional intelligence...

Options:

1. is set at birth and remains the same over time.
2. can grow and develop.

Answer:

Actually, emotional intelligence can grow and develop with age. In order to increase your emotional intelligence, it's important to understand the source of this brainpower.

Option 1: This answer is incorrect. Emotional intelligence is not set at birth and does not remain the same over time; rather it can grow and develop over time.

Option 2: This answer is correct. Emotional intelligence can grow and develop because life experiences and beliefs affect constructive thinking.

In this lesson, you'll learn how life experiences affect constructive thinking and how the thinking can change.

You'll learn why people form beliefs and how these beliefs can affect your thinking style.

Understanding the source of emotional intelligence is important to forming a strong sense of why you think the way you do.

All people have belief systems. They can vary widely from superstitions to practical ideas. Why do beliefs develop?

People develop belief systems to protect themselves and function in the world. You'll explore:
- the basic human needs,
- how beliefs relate to needs,
- the role beliefs play.

The first two human needs are simple. People strive to have pleasant, happy events in their lives. They also want to feel connected to the world.

See each need for more information.

Happiness

People strive to maximize pleasure and minimize pain. This is a basic human motivation. People want to be happy and avoid frustrating situations.

Relationships

People also want to have close relationships with others. They want to form friendships and other types of bonds.

Review each element for more information on how this belief system helps provide structure for Annette.

Predictability

"Because I am a good person, mostly good things will happen to me. I know that things will work out for the best for me and I'll have few bad experiences. I have a general idea of how my life will be because I'm a good person."

Meaning
"The world makes sense to me because people basically get what they deserve. It's not random. Bad things don't happen to people who don't earn them. Good people have positive experiences and lead rewarding lives. This makes sense to me."

Control
"My actions determine what will happen to me. I have control over my future. If I act appropriately, good things will happen to me. Bad events are a punishment for bad things I've done. I can limit my negative experiences by being a good person."

People want to understand the world they live in. This is why beliefs develop. Your belief system provides structure--it helps you understand information and apply it to the world.

Annette's belief system is based on the idea that good things happen to good people and bad things happen to bad people.

Annette's belief system helps her make choices and behave effectively in the world. They also help her make sense of life. Because she believes that "good" people have rewarding lives, the world is predictable and meaningful. She's able to control life according to her belief system. This makes life seem less chaotic and random. Annette's beliefs also protect her self-esteem. As long as good things are happening to her, she can have a positive self-image.

Belief systems are individual and can be shaken if they are challenged. If Annette experiences a tragic event, she'll have to decide whether her belief system is flawed or accept that she's a "bad" person.

Lance and Annette discussed her belief system.

Lance: People often interpret events to fit in with their belief systems. Do you ever see yourself doing that?

Annette: I guess so. When something bad happens to a person I know, I immediately try to think of something she's done to earn the problem.

Lance: How about when something good happens?

Annette: I think about what the person has done to deserve good experiences.

Lance: Often, belief systems become self-fulfilling prophecies. How do you think that applies to you?

Annette: I take a lot of positive action in my life because I believe it makes me a better person. These kinds of actions probably help me avoid many problems.

Lance and Annette discussed some principle foundations of beliefs. These systems aren't based on facts. Annette admitted that she interprets events to fit in with her belief system. She also admitted that the way she acts reaffirms rather than challenges her belief system. Like many people, Annette acts in a way that reaffirms what she thinks should happen.

Question

Practice what you've learned. What are the human needs that cause people to develop belief systems?

Options:

1. They want to maximize pleasure and minimize pain.
2. They want to find meaning in events.
3. They want to see the world as chaotic.
4. They want to maintain distance from other people.
5. They want to protect their self-esteem.

Answer:

Actually, people develop beliefs because they want to maximize pleasure and minimize pain. They want to find meaning in the world, protect their self-esteem, and have close emotional relationships with others.

Option 1: This choice is correct. People develop belief systems because they want to maximize pleasure and minimize pain, which is a basic human motivation. People want to be happy and avoid frustrating situations.

Option 2: This answer is correct. People develop belief systems because they want to find meaning in events. They are able to control life according to their belief systems, which makes life seem less chaotic and random.

Option 3: This answer is incorrect. If people wanted to see the world as chaotic, they would not develop belief systems because belief systems maintain order.

Option 4: This answer is incorrect. Human needs include people needing to feel connected to the world. People want to maintain close relationships with others rather than maintaining their distance from other people.

Option 5: This is a correct choice. One human need that causes people to develop belief system is the protection of self-esteem because as long as expected things are happening, individuals can have a positive self-image.

Beliefs help people understand the world. Beliefs come from basic human needs, including the needs to find meaning in life and control events.

Belief systems aren't based on facts and vary greatly from person to person.

Can a negative thinker become a positive thinker? Or do people generally stay the same over time?

People can grow and adapt depending on their experiences and the types of mental attitudes they possess.

Many factors play into a person's ability to think positively. You'll explore:
- how thinking normally maintains itself,
- why thinking skills can change after extreme events.

There are two kinds of thinkers--destructive thinkers and constructive thinkers. Constructive thinkers make life easier on themselves. They look at themselves positively and don't torture themselves when things go wrong.

See each type of thinking for more information.

Constructive Thinking

Constructive thinkers attribute positive events to their own character traits. They tend to attribute negative events to luck.

Destructive Thinking

Destructive thinkers blame themselves when things go wrong, but they don't give themselves credit for positive events.

You might think that people would switch to constructive thinking because the results are positive. Thinking styles are complex and learned through the events each person experiences.

See each aspect of why people think as they do for more information.

Why constructive thinking persists

People keep a positive thinking style because it works. People who expect the best often experience good things. Good thinkers often grow in constructive thinking skills over time. Older people often exhibit extremely strong constructive thinking skills.

Why destructive thinking persists

Negative thinking persists because it decreases disappointment. If you expect the worst, you won't feel let down when bad things happen. You never expected a positive event. Destructive thinking tends to maintain itself over time.

Why people don't change

Thinking is a learned behavior. It's difficult for people to change their thinking skills because their ideas have been learned from the events they experience. This is especially true for negative thinking. What you learn out of fear of punishment is very difficult to unlearn.

Events can change the way you think. Lynne used to be a negative thinker. Chuck was once a positive thinker. Because of the events they experienced, their thinking styles underwent a dramatic change.

See each heading to learn about the events Lynne and Chuck experienced and how it changed their thinking styles.

Lynne's Event

"About a year ago, I received a sudden promotion at work. I was able to buy the home I've always wanted. I also got married. The last year has been extremely positive for me."

Lynne's Thinking

"I used to be a negative person, but now I expect good things to happen. I feel positive about myself and I think that I deserve good things in life. I now believe that bad things are just bad luck."

Chuck's Event

"Last year, I was laid off from my firm. I've had trouble finding work. To top it all off, I was recently diagnosed with cancer. It's supposedly curable, but after the year I've had, I don't believe it."

Chuck's Thinking

"I used to be a positive person, but not anymore. I don't think a good attitude makes a difference.

I feel like I'm on a roller coaster going straight downhill with no end in sight. I expect the worst-- that way, at least I'm not disappointed."

Lynne and Chuck each underwent a change in their thinking styles. They both experienced common reactions. Chuck was once a positive person, but his confidence was shaken and his beliefs were challenged in a very negative way. The same thing happened to Lynne, but the event and the results were positive. Extreme events, whether positive or negative, can have a dramatic effect on a person's thinking style.

Question

Practice what you've learned. How does constructive thinking change with age?

Options:

1. Most people improve their constructive thinking skills as they age.

2. People who experience extremely negative events tend to think less constructively.

3. Constructive thinking skills never decrease.

4. People who experience traumatic events cannot think constructively.

Answer:

Actually, constructive thinking skills tend to improve with age, unless a person experiences severe trauma. However, some people are able to think constructively about destructive events.

Option 1: This answer is correct. Most people improve their constructive thinking skills as they age because positive attitudes are built over time and persist as they are reinforced.

Option 2: Correct. People who experience extremely negative events tend to think less constructively because if you expect the worst, you won't feel let down when bad things happen. They don't believe a good attitude makes a difference.

Option 3: This answer is incorrect. If constructive thinking skills never decreased, then negative events would have no effect on thought processes.

Option 4: This answer is incorrect. People who experienced traumatic events can think constructively with age, and they can rise to the challenge of overcoming adversity.

Thinking styles tend to maintain themselves. Constructive thinkers build their positive attitudes over time, while destructive thinkers tend to keep a negative outlook.

Thinking systems usually only change during dramatically positive or negative events. A destructive event can have positive results when a person rises to the challenge of overcoming adversity.

Eric was raised in an abusive home environment. He struggled a great deal during his younger years. Today, he is a successful salesman. How did he do it?

Eric has strong constructive thinking skills, which helped him move past a bad start and build a promising future. Many people survive deprived childhoods to build rewarding lives for themselves. In this topic, you'll explore:

- the similar characteristics of people who are able to overcome negative environments,
- the behaviors these survivors share.

Many people come from negative backgrounds. Some of these people are able to leave their pasts behind and move toward a brighter future. The coping skills these "survivors" exhibit are effective in managing other life problems.

See each type of esteem for more information on the effect of bad environments.

Low self-esteem

One of the most lasting effects of a bad childhood is low self-esteem. People see themselves as "bad" to avoid blaming or resenting their parents or caretakers.

Healthy self-esteem

Survivors manage to retain their self-esteem. Even though they receive constant negative feedback, they don't see themselves as "bad."

Eric has overcome a negative childhood environment to build a strong career and a rewarding personal life. He is a survivor. There are other people out there like Eric. These survivors share some similar characteristics.

Review each characteristic for a description of the traits that Eric exhibits as a survivor, as related by Shari, a workplace counselor.

Acceptance

"Eric accepts himself and others. He doesn't try to change people and he basically likes who he is. He isn't jealous of other people's lives and he doesn't want to be anyone other than himself. This helps him accept the things he has to deal with."

Independence

"Eric doesn't rely on others to solve his problems for him. He takes charge of his own life. Because he is so independent, he is also not likely to blame others for how things turn out. He takes the initiative to make positive changes in his life."

Optimism

"Eric is fundamentally an optimist. He expects good things to happen instead of waiting for negative events. He sees the good qualities that other people possess. He plans for the future with the mind-set that there will be good things down the road."

Trust

"Even though Eric has dealt with negative circumstances, he still finds people he can trust. He doesn't shut himself off from contact. He reaches out to others and also asks for help when he needs it. He doesn't try to do everything by himself--he looks to people he knows he can trust."

Resilience

"Eric was able to overcome a negative past because he is resilient. He's not easily defeated. When bad things happen, he takes a problem-solving attitude rather than a defeated stance. He is able to be hopeful rather than losing his drive in depressing thoughts."

Shari is going to talk with Nick, who recently experienced personal crises including a divorce and a bad car accident.

Shari talked with Nick about how he overcame a difficult past.

Shari: What are some actions you took to overcome the difficulties you faced in life?

Nick: I found a mentor, someone who helped me through the bad times. My friend Chris has overcome some bad experiences. I talked to him about my problems and he gave me advice.

Shari: How did you avoid losing hope?

Nick: I tried to remember that good things happened to me too, instead of just focusing on the negative events. Every day, I thought about something good that happened and spent time thinking about the positive event.

Shari: Are there any other ways you helped yourself during your difficult time?

Nick: I tried to remember that bad things weren't happening because I was a bad person. Bad things happen to everyone. I couldn't take the blame for events that were out of my control.

Nick exhibits many of the qualities of a survivor. He didn't let his bad experiences cloud his view of life. He kept a big-picture outlook and had hope that things would improve. He also found a mentor, which is key to self-esteem during times of difficulty.

Question

Practice what you've learned. Select the coping skills often displayed by those who survive deprived environments.

Options:

1. They keep a big-picture outlook.
2. They see themselves as "bad" when they receive negative feedback.
3. They are independent.
4. They are optimistic.
5. They don't preserve their self-esteem.

Answer:

Actually, coping skills include keeping a big-picture outlook, being independent and optimistic, and preserving self-esteem.

Option 1: Correct. One coping skill displayed by those who survive deprived environments is keeping a big-picture outlook. They don't let bad experiences cloud their view of life. If bad things do happen, they hope that things will improve.

Option 2: This answer is incorrect. People who survive destructive environments do not see themselves as "bad," even though they received negative feedback. Rather survivors manage to retain their self-esteem.

Option 3: This answer is correct. A coping skill often displayed by those who survive deprived environments is independence. They take charge of their own lives. Because they are independent, they are not likely to blame others for how things turn out.

Option 4: Correct. Another coping skill of survivors is optimism. They expect good things to happen and see the good qualities that other people possess. They plan for the future with the mind-set that there will be good things down the road.

Option 5: This answer is incorrect. Survivors preserve their self-esteem, and have the resilience needed to cope during difficult times.

Many people experience negative or deprived environments in which they get a lot of bad feedback and little positive reinforcement. There are resilient people who are able to survive these experiences and build rewarding lives for themselves. These "survivors" are able to build their own self-esteem and turn to others to find the reinforcement they need to feel good about themselves.

IMPROVING YOUR EMOTIONAL INTELLIGENCE

Improving Your Emotional Intelligence

What if you found a way to improve your career? Your personal life? Would you try to make a positive change?

There is a way to make a positive impact on your career and personal life. You can improve your emotional intelligence. There are documented techniques to improve your mind in this way. You'll explore:
- why it's important to be aware of your emotions,
- how you can evaluate your thought process,
- what you can do to improve the way you think.

In this section, you'll be given the tools to increase your emotional intelligence. You'll learn proven techniques for improving the way you feel.

Have you ever asked yourself, "Why do I let other people get to me?" Have you ever tried to talk yourself out of a bad mood?

It can be difficult to talk yourself out of bad feelings. Why? Because feelings come from a different part of your mind than logic. Emotions come from the experiential

mind; logic and rational thoughts come from the logical mind. In this topic, you'll examine:
- how the experiential mind learns
- where emotions come from
- how to begin tuning in to your emotional mind.

There is a series of steps that takes place between an event and a behavioral response. During these steps, your emotions develop as you interpret the event or events that took place. Your interpretations are a major factor in the response you make.

See each stage for information about the steps involved in a reaction.

You interpret the event

The event occurs and you interpret it. Suppose your co-worker, Jane, sits down at her desk and doesn't speak to you all day, which is unusual. There are many possible interpretations, ranging from, "Jane's upset about something personal," to, "Jane's mad at me."

You react to the interpretation with an emotional response

You will have an emotional response based on the event. If you think Jane is having personal problems, you may respond with sympathy. If you think Jane's angry at you, you may begin to feel angry in return.

You may then have follow-up interpretations

If your initial interpretation is, "Jane's angry at me," your follow-up might be, "That's silly; Jane doesn't have any reason to be angry at me. Maybe she's just tired because she's under a lot of pressure right now."

The follow-up interpretations may produce a change in your emotion

After a follow-up interpretation, your emotions might change. If you decide that Jane is withdrawing because of deadline pressure instead of anger at you, your emotion may change from anger to sympathy.

You may have a reaction

You may have a behavioral reaction depending on your interpretation. If you feel angry at Jane, you may act cold or snap at her. If you feel sympathy, you may offer to help her or act in another way that might soothe her.

No matter what emotions you feel, you have the option to react in a variety of ways. Imagine that your boss makes a sharp remark to you during a meeting. Because you interpret the event to mean that your boss thinks badly of you, your reaction is to become angry. However, you decide not to visibly react.

This is damage control. You're still experiencing the emotion, but you've controlled your action. Is this solving the problem?

If you've interpreted an event in a destructive way, coping reactions are damage control. The emotion still causes stress. The best way to deal with bad emotions is to learn about the interpretations you make and why they may cause problems.

So how can you find out more about your feelings? It's important to pay close attention to what goes on in your mind. It's easiest to notice your thought process when you're reacting emotionally.

Review each thought process for more information about how to become aware of your experiential mind.

Self talk

When you're emotional, tune in to what you're saying to yourself. You may hear things like, "I'm such an idiot!" or, "What a jerk!"

Mental Images

You will often see visual images or vague impressions in your mind when you are upset. You might "see red" when you're angry.

During the exercise, you saw how interpretations can lead to specific emotions. If you become aware of your interpretations, you can start to understand why you feel the way you do.

Question

Practice what you've learned. Sequence the chain of events that takes place between an event and a behavioral reaction.

Options:

A. You interpret the event.

B. You react to the interpretation with an emotional response.

C. You may then have follow-up interpretations.

D. The follow-up interpretations may produce a change in your emotion.

E. You may then have a behavioral reaction.

Answer:

Actually, you first interpret the event and react emotionally. Your follow-up interpretations may change your emotions. Finally, you visibly react.

Correct answer(s):

You interpret the event. is ranked The first step in the sequence. This is the first step that takes place between an event and a behavioral reaction. When you interpret the event, you determine your initial reaction to what happened.

You react to the interpretation with an emotional response. is ranked The second step in the sequence. The second step is to react to the interpretation with an emotional response. This response is based on the event and how you initially view it.

You may then have follow-up interpretations. is ranked The third step in the sequence. The third step may be to have follow-up interpretations. You may change your interpretation of the event after some thought.

The follow-up interpretations may produce a change in your emotion. is ranked The fourth step in the sequence. The fourth step is that follow-up interpretations may produce a change in your emotion if you think your follow-up interpretation is more logical or accurate.

You may then have a behavioral reaction. is ranked The fifth step in the sequence. The final step is that you may have a behavioral reaction. Depending on the interpretation you determine to be most accurate, you may or may not react to the situation.

It's difficult to apply logical, rational thought to emotions. These feelings are caused by steps that affect your reaction. To understand why you have each emotion, you must know the interpretations you make.

In order to learn more about why you feel the way you do, you must begin listening to your experiential mind.

On Monday morning, Calvin, an administrative assistant, stopped by Robin's office to ask for her commission report. Robin snapped at Calvin, saying the report wasn't ready and he'd just have to wait.

Calvin was furious. He got the impression Robin didn't think his time was valuable. Was he wrong to think that?

Was Calvin wrong? He interpreted an event. Interpretations aren't right or wrong. However, these assessments can be either destructive or constructive. Calvin's was destructive because it lead to anger at Robin. You'll examine:

- why it's important to make constructive interpretations,
- how you can assess the constructiveness of your interpretations,
- how you can evaluate your behavior.

Your initial interpretation has the strongest effect on your emotions. Interpretations aren't right or wrong, but they can be constructive or destructive.

See each employee to find out what they're thinking, and then select the corresponding analysis of their interpretations to find out if they're correct in their assumptions.

Jay

"My boss asked me when I'd finish the report I'm preparing. Now I'm panicking because I think he wants it earlier. I was supposed to have three more days to finish it, but he must want it as soon as possible if he asked about it."

Reading too much in

Jay is reading too much into his boss's question about the deadline. His boss doesn't necessarily want the report early just because he asked a question. Jay's interpretation is causing a great deal of anxiety.

Lisa

"I met Ned, the new project manager, the other day. He was extremely unpleasant during a team meeting on Monday morning. I can tell by this meeting that he's a real jerk. I'm going to hate working with him.

Making generalizations

Lisa is making a generalization about Ned based on one meeting. He may have had a bad morning or received unpleasant news. Ned may be a very likeable person who is just having a bad day.

Michelle

"One of the women in my office got a bunch of people together for lunch the other day. I was in a meeting and I didn't hear about the lunch until the afternoon. I know she just wanted to leave me out."

"My boss asked me when I'd finish the report I'm preparing. Now I'm panicking because I think he wants it earlier. I was supposed to have three more days to finish it, but he must want it as soon as possible if he asked about it."

Making assumptions

Michelle is assuming that her co-worker had negative intentions. The woman may have just overlooked her because she wasn't in the office during the morning. She probably didn't have any desire to leave Michelle out.

Rick

"I applied for tuition reimbursement for a foreign language course. The request was denied by my vice president. She obviously doesn't think I'm a worthwhile employee since she won't put any effort into developing me."

Taking it personally

Rick is personalizing this event. His tuition reimbursement request may have been denied because of budget problems or timing. He's assuming that he was denied for personal reasons and ignoring the other factors that may be involved.

During the follow-up interpretation, you assess your initial interpretation and make adjustments. There are some common pitfalls for this interpretation. They include:
- blaming yourself. "That person is being rude because I'm an idiot."
- denying facts you don't want to believe. "I couldn't have hurt his feelings."
- thinking unrealistically. "I'll figure it out somehow. I don't need any help."

The final step in a response to an event is your behavioral reaction. These responses, like interpretations, can be destructive or constructive.

Review the examples of destructive behavioral reactions to learn more.

Aggression

Aggression is a very common destructive behavior. The aggressor lashes out or attacks others during times of high emotion. Although aggression is appropriate in some cases, it often alienates or angers other people.

Uninhibited expression

Some people choose to express their emotions freely without any control. They don't consider the consequences of showing strong emotions to other people. This kind of "free expression" can alienate others and hurt other people's feelings. It can also lead to embarrassment.

Overcontrolled expression

Some people reign in their emotions so much that they don't even seem to have feelings at all. They appear cold and withdrawn to others. People can't figure out how they feel or what their opinions are. This type of control leads to avoiding the resolution of problems.

Self-punishment

Some people punish themselves when they feel they've done something bad. They might feel extreme guilt or deny themselves pleasurable experiences. They may also force themselves to do things they don't like to "atone" for bad behavior.

Overdependence

It's perfectly acceptable to ask for help or advice. However, some people rely too much on others. They don't have enough self-esteem to accomplish goals on their own. Overdependence is destructive to relationships and can cause self-esteem to drop even more.

Extreme self-reliance

Some people are overly independent. They refuse to allow others to help or advise them. It makes other people feel inferior. This extreme self-reliance is also a source of stress. Everyone needs help sometimes and it's OK to enlist others in some situations.

Withdrawal

When you withdraw, you stop participating. Withdrawal can be appropriate in some situations, but can be damaging if overused. It puts distance between you and others and makes it difficult to form relationships.

Stacy and Sean discussed constructive and destructive behavior.

Stacy: Sometimes, destructive behaviors can actually be constructive.

Sean: It seems like destructive behavior would be destructive in any context. Can you give me an example of when a destructive behavior is constructive?

Stacy: Sure. Aggression, such as physical assault, is extremely destructive at work. But if you're being attacked or physically threatened, aggression on your part is completely appropriate.

Sean: That makes sense. Can you give me another example?

Stacy: Withdrawal can be appropriate if you need to get away for a short period of time. If you've been extremely offended or are highly emotional, you may need to disengage for a while to calm down.

Stacy explained that context is extremely important to evaluating behavior. The context provides a framework. Most destructive behaviors are only constructive in extreme or rare circumstances. Aggression is rarely appropriate, but is a constructive response if you're being assaulted. Most destructive behaviors are only constructive in the short term as coping mechanisms.

Question

Practice what you've learned. Identify some key areas of appraisal in judging the constructiveness or destructiveness of a reaction.

Options:

1. Evaluate the constructiveness of the initial interpretation.

2. Determine how positive the initial interpretation is.

3. Evaluate the behavior reaction in the context in which it occurred.

4. Assess your initial interpretation and adjust accordingly.

Answer:
Actually, you should evaluate the constructiveness of the initial interpretation, the follow-up interpretation, and the behavior reaction. Context is important to an accurate evaluation.

Option 1: This answer is correct. One key area of appraisal is to evaluate the constructiveness of the initial interpretation because your initial interpretation has the strongest effect on your emotions.

Option 2: This answer is incorrect. The initial interpretation does not necessarily need to be positive because a negative reaction may be appropriate.

Option 3: This choice is correct. You should evaluate the behavior reaction in the context in which it occurred because context provides a framework. Depending on the situation, a destructive reaction might be appropriate.

Option 4: This answer is correct. Another key area of appraisal is to assess your initial interpretation and adjust accordingly because your initial interpretation may be off base.

When you evaluate your experiential self, it's important to consider your initial interpretations, your follow-up interpretations, and your behavioral reaction. Each of these can be assessed for constructive or destructive components.

It's important to consider context when making these evaluations. Context is the key to appropriate evaluation.

You know that increasing your emotional intelligence is important. What can you do to increase this type of brainpower?

Increasing your emotional intelligence can reduce stress and improve relationships. There are three proven

techniques for retraining your mind. You'll examine tools that will help you:
- train your emotions through logic,
- correct inappropriate emotional responses,
- learn from your emotions.

The techniques available for training your experiential mind are very different approaches. Some tools will work for some people; other tools are a better match for other people. The technique that works best for you depends on the problems you experience. You should experiment with each strategy to increase your emotional intelligence.

The first technique you can use is to train your experiential mind using logical, rational thought. This is a process, and your skills will develop over time.

See the steps in training your experiential mind to use logical, rational thought for more information.

1. Assess interpretations

First, you must identify the ways in which your interpretations are constructive or destructive. You can do this by writing down your initial and follow-up interpretations and reactions, and assessing each.

2. Substitute

Second, you must substitute destructive interpretations and behaviors with constructive ones. Generate a list of constructive alternatives. At first, you'll only think of these options after the destructive response occurs.

3. Identify occasions

Third, you'll need to identify the times you tend to have destructive responses. This pattern will become apparent after you've tracked your reactions over time. You might notice that when you're tired or stressed, destructive responses increase.

4. Begin to change

The final step will occur over time. At last, the substitution of constructive interpretations and behaviors will become automatic. Your thought process will improve and you'll find that your emotions become more productive.

The next technique you can use is to correct emotions logically. In this approach, you work backward after you've experienced an emotion. You logically analyze, then dispute the emotion.

Jessica is going to work with Tim to dispute a difficult emotion using this technique. Tim and Jessica discussed logically correcting emotions.

Tim: I've been worrying nonstop about my project deadline. I keep thinking something will happen to make me miss it.

Jessica: How does that thinking about missing the deadline make you feel?

Tim: Awful! I lie awake at night tossing and turning.

Jessica: What would happen if you didn't worry like that?

Tim: I don't know. I guess I'd feel like I wasn't taking the project seriously.

Jessica: What if you changed your approach? You planned your work, but then didn't allow yourself to worry. Would anything happen?

Tim: I guess not. The worry itself is a habit. It's just holding me back.

To correct yourself with this approach, you need to reframe your thoughts. This means changing the way you think. First, you must accept your current emotional state. Then you must decide how you'd like things to be. Finally, you should generate a list of actions that will help you meet your goal. This process will help you look forward to an improved emotional state.

The final technique you can use doesn't involve steps or procedures. It involves listening to your emotions. Have you ever gotten a bad feeling about a decision or an action? Often, these emotions correspond to concrete facts or reasons. By listening to yourself, you may improve your behavior.

- When you have "bad vibes," ask yourself, "What's causing this feeling?"
- You may find that you have bad feelings when you're uncomfortable for a logical reason.

Question

Practice what you've learned. Identify the three approaches for improving constructive thinking.

Options:

1. Use the logical mind to change the way the experiential mind works.

2. Re-frame destructive interpretations.

3. Learn from emotional reactions.

4. Ignore emotional reactions.

Answer:

Actually, the three approaches for improving constructive thinking include using the logical mind to change the experiential mind, re-framing destructive interpretations, and learning from emotions.

Option 1: Correct. One approach for improving constructive thinking is to use the logical mind to change the way the experiential mind works. You work backward after you've experienced an emotion. You logically analyze, and then dispute the emotion.

Option 2: Correct. Another approach is to re-frame destructive interpretations. You must accept your current emotional state, decide how you would like things to be, and generate a list of actions that will help you meet your goal.

Option 3: Correct. An approach for improving constructive thinking is to learn from emotional reactions. Often your emotions correspond to concrete facts or reasons. By listening to yourself, you may improve your behavior.

Option 4: This answer is incorrect. Ignoring your emotional reactions is not an approach for improving constructive thinking. By ignoring your emotional reactions, you may miss a very real and logical response to a situation.

By training your experiential mind, you can increase your emotional intelligence. There are three basic techniques you can use.

- You can train your experiential mind through logic.
- You can correct inappropriate emotional responses.
- You can listen to your emotions.

Almost every career you can think of involves interacting with other people--whether it's working side by side or dealing with customers. By increasing your emotional intelligence, you'll be able to improve your relationships with others. You'll also decrease your stress level by improving your thought process.

CHAPTER V - EMOTIONALLY INTELLIGENT LEADERSHIP

CHAPTER V - Emotionally Intelligent Leadership

Emotional intelligence is a popular concept. How does it relate to your effectiveness as a leader?

This chapter delves into the importance of emotional intelligence to today's leaders. You'll examine:
- why leaders need emotional intelligence,
- how you can acquire emotional intelligence,
- why it's important to develop your staff,
- how you can increase others' emotional intelligence.

THE NEED FOR EMOTIONALLY INTELLIGENT LEADERS

The Need for Emotionally Intelligent Leaders

"Leadership is not a position. You are not a leader because you have the title of manager. Leadership is something that we earn from followers on a day-to-day basis." --The EMS Manager Newsletter

What makes someone a great leader? There are many factors, but emotional intelligence is recognized as an important factor for leading others to success. In this lesson, you'll explore:
- why emotional intelligence is becoming more important to leadership,
- how this type of brainpower is valuable to leaders,
- what the key attributes of emotionally intelligent leaders are.

The workplace is changing as technology makes business more global. Employees, communication systems, products, and customers are becoming more and more complex every day. Today's executives must be able to manage relationships effectively to realize success. By developing your emotional intelligence, you'll be able to achieve new heights.

"The work world is changing rapidly," says Peter, the CEO of a large finance firm. "I need leaders who can effectively respond to change."

Peter is expressing a common concern of leaders everywhere. The workplace is changing rapidly. The necessary leadership skills are evolving as well. Today's executives need to motivate others and adapt quickly. In this topic, you'll learn:

- the trends that are changing today's work world,
- how these changes affect leadership,
- why emotional intelligence helps leaders navigate change.

Question

Which trends are significantly affecting the business world?

Options:

1. electronic communication
2. changes in the structure of corporations
3. advances in technologies
4. telecommuting
5. increased globalization of companies

Answer:

Actually, all of these trends and advances have significantly affected the way we do business.

Option 1: This answer is correct. Electronic communication is a trend that is significantly affecting the business world because there are now a number of ways in which individuals can communicate with one another.

Option 2: Correct. Changes in the structure of corporations significantly affects the business world.

Organizational structure is shifting from strict upward hierarchical configurations to more decentralized, flat structures.

Option 3: This answer is correct. Advances in technologies are significantly affecting the business world because of shifts in communication channels and new kinds of products and services.

Option 4: This answer is correct. Telecommuting is significantly affecting the business world because the workforce no longer needs to be in a centralized area.

Option 5: This answer is correct. The increased globalization of companies affects the business world because companies no longer have to rely only on local customers. Today, buyers can be found around the globe.

Technology has made a significant difference in business life. Office environments are evolving because of shifts in communication channels. Customers can choose from new kinds of products and services.

See each business activity for more information about changes that result from technology.

Communication

Communication has changed through technologies. Videoconferences are more frequent than meetings. E-mail has replaced memos.

Production

Through new innovations, products can be created faster and cheaper. Product life cycles are reduced when new inventions replace old tools.

There are other important changes occurring in today's workplace. These shifts have a significant effect on how products and services are created and marketed.

Review each aspect for more information on the transformations that are taking place.

Geography

The Internet makes it possible for people to communicate across thousands of miles within seconds. No company has to rely only on local customers. Today, buyers can be found around the globe.

Demographics

Market boundaries used to be strictly drawn. A salesperson might be assigned to the Southwest or Northeast. Today, market lines are blurred. Salespeople market to demographics rather than territories.

Regulations

As more governments become involved in industry, more regulations spring up. These rules are further complicated by technology. It can be difficult to keep up with and implement all these regulatory requirements.

Leadership

Corporations are changing with the times. Organizational structure is shifting from strict upward hierarchical configurations to more decentralized, flat structures. This means there are fewer formal leaders in many companies.

Stephanie asked Peter about how the changing workplace affects leadership.

Stephanie: How do you think changes in the global market have changed the skills leaders need?

Peter: There are a lot of ways. For one thing, workers are changing. They don't expect to have the same job for 30 years. They change jobs more frequently.

Stephanie: How do leaders need to respond to these changes?

Peter: They need to develop their employees in order to motivate them. People want to build a diverse set of skills so they are employable in the future. They look for development opportunities.

Stephanie: What are some other changes leaders face?

Peter: They need to be extremely flexible. Change happens fast today. I need strong leaders who can adapt rather than fight change.

Stephanie: How can leaders ensure that they are successful?

Peter: They need to understand that customer service is the key. Lots of companies make similar products, so customer service is what separates the winners from the losers.

Emotional intelligence is a person's ability to solve problems, work effectively with others, and make sense of the world around him. This type of brainpower is critical to leadership in the evolving business world.

Leaders need to be flexible enough to adapt to change. They also need the skills to motivate others--not only face-to-face, but through multiple forms of communication.

Question

Practice what you've learned. What are the trends in today's business world that make executive emotional intelligence important?

Options:

1. Market boundaries are more rigid.
2. Changes in regulations have become simpler and less frequent.
3. Product life cycles are shorter.
4. Customer satisfaction is becoming more critical.

5. Organizations are becoming more decentralized.

Answers:

Actually, trends that are changing the business world include shorter product life cycles, the increased importance of customer satisfaction, and decentralized organizations.

Option 1: This choice is incorrect. If market boundaries were more rigid, there would be less of a need for emotionally intelligent executives because lines would be strictly drawn.

Option 2: This answer is incorrect. If changes in regulations were simpler and less frequent, there would be less need for emotionally intelligent leaders because it would be easy to keep up with and implement all the regulatory requirements.

Option 3: Correct. Shorter product lifecycles make emotional intelligence important because through new innovations, products can be created faster and cheaper. Product life cycles are reduced when new inventions replace old tools.

Option 4: Correct. Customer satisfaction is becoming critical, which makes emotional intelligence important because executives need to understand that what separates one company from another is the service that goes with the product.

Option 5: Correct. Because organizations are becoming more decentralized, executive emotional intelligence is increasingly important since there are fewer formal leaders in many companies.

As the workplace changes, leaders need to adapt their skills. As the marketplace becomes increasingly global and companies decentralize, a new breed of successful leaders will emerge. These executives will be able to adapt rapidly to change. They'll be able to motivate employees to achieve complex goals. These leaders will be able to meet the challenges of tomorrow.

How do you know if a leader is effective? What results can emotionally intelligent executives achieve?

Emotionally intelligent leaders can provide value in many ways. These leaders share common traits and achieve similar results, regardless of their industries. You'll examine:
- the benefits emotionally intelligent leaders provide,
- how these benefits affect customers and employees.

The work force has changed. Twenty years ago, a manager handed out assignments to individuals. Now, teams are becoming more common. An important skill for leaders is the ability to put together the right teams and motivate them to accomplish goals.

See each attribute for more information on teams.

Flattened structure

Top-down, hierarchical companies used to dominate business. Today, organizations are becoming flat and fewer clear leaders exist.

Blend of skills

Effective leaders build strong teams that accomplish goals. These teams don't rely on power structures, but on a strong blend of skills.

No good leader can ignore profits or the bottom line. Many average leaders are able to achieve results that can be boiled down to dollars and cents. The best leaders accomplish financial goals in addition to providing other types of value.

See each contribution leaders can make for more information.

integrity

Leaders with integrity help build customer loyalty. Consumers are becoming more aware of corporations' social responsibility. They want companies to make products and stand behind them. They avoid companies that abuse the environment and their customers.

openness to learning

Learning doesn't stop when a college degree is earned. Good leaders encourage learning throughout their organizations. This "openness to learning" helps the company be responsive. Employees know more about their environment and the actions they can take to be successful.

results across the organization

A good leader doesn't just accomplish results in his department. He affects the organization as a whole. He sets goals that benefit the company, not just himself or his team. Effective leaders team with vendors and other departments to benefit everyone's bottom line.

accountability

Have you ever heard the expression, "The buck stops here"? This describes the attitude of a mature, professional leader. These executives accept responsibility, hold themselves to high standards, and stand behind their commitments.

Don and Joyce discussed her boss's leadership style.

Don: How do you think your boss has increased customer satisfaction for the branch of your bank?

Joyce: He stands behind our products and the customers know it. He'll take responsibility when a mistake is made. He doesn't blame a teller--he just makes sure the problem gets solved.

Don: There's very little turnover at your branch. How does your boss hold on to employees?

Joyce: Working for him is a great opportunity. He encourages us to learn and improve our skills. He also makes sure the right people are in the right jobs.

Don: Does he help employees get along with each other?

Joyce: Yes. We used to compete to see which teller was the "best." Now we've learned that we're all a team. If we support each other, we can all be successful. Don: How has your boss contributed to the bank as a whole?

Joyce: Our branch is successful, which helps the bottom line. Our tellers are skilled enough to train new workers at other branches. Everyone benefits, not just our branch.

Joyce's boss has provided value in a number of ways. His employees are skilled, so his branch is profitable. These workers are available to train new hires at other branches, so the bank as a whole benefits. He encourages his employees to act as a team. He fosters continuous learning and aligns the team so that the right people are in the right jobs. He displays many of the characteristics of effective leaders.

Question
Practice what you've learned. Which are areas of value provided by the emotionally intelligent leader?

Options:
1. focusing on profits

2. building hierarchies
3. communicating
4. building teams
5. positioning resources

Answers:

Actually, emotionally intelligent leaders build teams, communicate, and position resources. They are also open to learning and provide results across the organization.

Option 1: Incorrect. Focusing on profits is not a value provided by an emotionally intelligent leader. An emotionally intelligent leader understands that by focusing only on profits, they will miss a number of opportunities to add value to the organization.

Option 2: This answer is incorrect. An emotionally intelligent leader does not build hierarchies because organizations are becoming flat and fewer clear leaders exist.

Option 3: This answer is correct. An emotionally intelligent leader provides value through effective communication throughout the company. They seek the input of all members to make effective decisions.

Option 4: Correct. Emotionally intelligent leaders provide value through effective team building because they understand that strong teams accomplish goals. These teams don't rely on power structures, but on a strong blend of skills.

Option 5: Correct. An emotionally intelligent leader provides value through positioning resources. They know the importance of positioning individuals to provide effective results so that the right people are in the right jobs.

Emotionally intelligent leaders provide value in a number of ways. They position their companies and employees to be successful in the future. These executives act with integrity and professional maturity.

The value these leaders provide increases both customer and employee loyalty. They achieve results across entire organizations.

Emotional intelligence is critical to good leadership. How can you develop the habits of good leaders?

Good leaders share several important attributes. Their emotional intelligence is reflected in their attitudes and behaviors. In this topic, you'll examine:

- why it's important to separate work and personal relationships,
- how confidence and appreciation improve leadership,
- why compromise is important,
- why taking responsibility is critical.

Emotionally intelligent executives must develop good relationships with their staff members. However, they must also keep an appropriate distance. They can't let personal friendships affect business. They shouldn't make staffing assignments or promotions based on nonbusiness relationships. When executives let personal feelings interfere at work, problems can arise--ranging from jealousy to serious errors.

Leaders can still have close personal relationships, but they must be very careful to keep these friendships separate from work. This can be difficult but is in everyone's best interests.

Good leaders must be able to take decisive action. They must also develop their employees to achieve success. See

each group to learn more about emotional intelligence and leadership.
Confident leaders
High self-esteem is critical to emotional intelligence. Confidence helps leaders make decisions and take action, even when they face disagreement.
Valued employees
Confident leaders must care enough about their employees to help people develop and contribute. They must appreciate the contributions others make.

Compromise can be difficult, especially when you know that your team or project will be affected. However, emotionally intelligent leaders know that compromise is essential to good business relationships. Ned recently had to make a decision regarding one of his staff members.

Explore each step, in order, to learn more about the process Ned went through to compromise.
Think through the situation
"I often run into situations that require tough decisions. For example, one staff member asked me for a vacation during the busiest time of the year. No one had ever asked for that before, so I had to think through the situation."
Look at past experiences
"The first thing I did was try to decide if the issue had been addressed in the past. There may be a policy that applies to the situation. However, in this case, it was an exception. The problem hadn't come up before, so I didn't have a policy."
Separate situation from effect
"I had to think about the situation separately from the effect. I give my employees a generous vacation package. I tell them it's important to recharge their batteries. This

person had never taken time off. If I had refused, I could have sent a mixed message."

Find a compromise

"I decided on a compromise--she could take part of the time off. That way, the effect to the team was minimal, but I wasn't depriving her of some vacation time. I made a decision that was a win-win situation."

Often, an executive has to take responsibility for serious decisions. To make the best decision possible, it's important to act carefully. Carey supervises a project team that's creating a computer system for an important client. The client has requested several changes that have affected the project budget seriously. Carey had to decide whether or not to approach the client for additional money.

See each task for more information on Carey's process.

Be directly involved

"I didn't rely on second-hand information from anyone. I met with the project team and sat in on meetings with the customer. That way, I knew firsthand what all the issues were. I didn't want to run into misunderstandings because of bad information."

Get all the information

"I found out everything I could. I familiarized myself with the budget, project timelines, the original proposal, and all change requests. I knew all the project expenditures by heart. There were no gaps in my knowledge. A well-informed decision was critical."

Be present during implementation

"I didn't hand off the decision to anyone else. I took care of it myself. When we asked for more money, I was present during all client negotiations. I didn't want someone else to feel like he or she had to justify my decision."

Question

Practice what you've learned. What are the key attributes of emotionally intelligent leaders?

Options:

1. keeping direct involvement
2. having the courage to never back down
3. having the ability to compromise when appropriate
4. relying on a set of informants to provide information.

Answer:

Actually, effective leaders stay involved. They're able to compromise when it's appropriate. They collect all available information when problems arise.

Option 1: This answer is correct. One of the key attributes of emotionally leaders is keeping direct involvement because knowing all the issues firsthand means there will not be misunderstandings due to bad information.

Option 2: Incorrect. This is not a key attribute of emotional intelligent leaders, because it can take just as much courage to back down. Compromise can bring about positive results.

Option 3: This answer is correct. An emotionally intelligent leader has the ability to compromise when appropriate because it is important in order to maintain good business relationships.

Option 4: This answer is incorrect. Emotionally intelligent leaders do not rely on informants to provide information because they know that second-hand knowledge can be misleading.

Emotionally intelligent leaders project confidence and build the self-esteem of their employees. They compromise when appropriate and take responsibility for their actions.

Remember that it's important to separate business and personal relationships. An appropriate level of distance will help you make sound decisions.

ACQUIRING EMOTIONAL INTELLIGENCE AS A LEADER

Acquiring Emotional Intelligence as a Leader

Studies show that the best leaders share some common characteristics. How do these qualities inspire employees?

When top leaders are studied, it's found that they share some common characteristics. These shared abilities aren't technical and don't include IQ. Instead, the best managers have developed "executive emotional intelligence." In this lesson, you'll explore what it means to:

- develop nonjudgmentalism, perception, and sincerity,
- take responsibility for problems,
- foster loyalty and motivate employees.

Question

Which are the benefits of acquiring emotional intelligence?

Options:

1. It will help you increase your technical skills.
2. It will help you be more productive.

3. It will help you build better relationships with others.
4. It will help you manage conflict.
5. It will help you cope with change.
6. It will help you deal with diversity.

Answers:

Actually, emotional intelligence can help you build better relationships, manage conflict, cope with change, and deal with diversity.

Option 1: This answer is incorrect. A benefit of acquiring emotionally intelligence is not to increase your technical skills, but to increase your people management skills.

Option 2: This answer is incorrect. Being emotionally intelligent may not help you be more productive, but it will definitely help your employees to be more productive.

Option 3: This answer is correct. Acquiring emotional intelligence will help you build better relationships with others because others will appreciate your ability to be accepting, honest, and sincere with them.

Option 4: This answer is correct. A benefit of acquiring emotional intelligence is it will help you manage conflict because you will be better equipped to deal with individuals on all levels.

Option 5: This answer is correct. One benefit of emotional intelligence is it will help you cope with change. Because change affects different people in different ways, you will be equipped to handle a variety of reactions in others and yourself.

Option 6: This answer is correct. Emotional intelligence will help you deal with diversity. You will be able to work with a wide variety of people and interact effectively with others.

In this lesson, you'll learn the qualities you need to acquire executive emotional intelligence. You'll build an understanding of the characteristics that the best leaders share.

You'll also learn how your attitude and intentions can affect your ability to lead and manage others.

How does a leader's attitude affect his or her management style? How can you make sure you look at your team members in a helpful way?

Your attitude toward your staff members determines how you will treat them. By making sure you value all workers, you'll improve your relationships with your staff. You'll explore:

- why it's important to avoid judgments,
- how your perception can help you manage,
- why sincerity is important.

Trevor is a senior-level manager in the processing division of a large bank. He has a good track record with his employees. His department experiences low turnover and most employees are satisfied and productive.

See each aspect to learn more about how Trevor approaches management.

Accept

"I accept each person on the basis of what he or she offers right now. I don't evaluate people on what may or may not have happened in the past. I also avoid listening to gossip about someone's past."

Respect

"Your employees respect you only if they know you respect them. I try to treat people with courtesy. I respect their skills and their personal lives as much as possible. They can sense that I value them and they appreciate it."

Avoid judgment
"It's easy to judge people, but it's not productive. When you're in management, it's important not to look down on people or evaluate them based on qualities that aren't work-related. Judgmental behavior hurts your relationship with your staff."

Support
"I support my team members as much as possible. I let them know I'm concerned about them. I also try to have compassion about the frustrations they face. I avoid saying things like, "Tough it out," because it trivializes their struggles."

Good leaders have a great deal of perception. They understand themselves and the people around them. They make better decisions about delegating projects, choosing teams, and assigning other working relationships because they understand how individuals think and feel.

Check each aspect to learn more about perception.

understanding yourself
It's very important that you understand your own strengths and weaknesses. To develop an accurate self-assessment, you must be open to feedback from other people. Consider the response you get from others. Seek information about yourself from people you trust.

understanding others
Good leaders understand other people's feelings. They make accurate assessments about why other people act and think the way they do. It's important that you observe others and learn about what they are feeling. This understanding will help you interact effectively with others.

using your perception

You can use your understanding of others to help them learn more about themselves. You must start with a sincere desire to help rather than a personal agenda to change someone. You should use feedback and reinforcement of positive action to help others learn about themselves.

Sincerity means being honest about both your feelings and your goals. If you're sincere, you communicate with your staff members about the direction you are taking, even when you know they won't be happy. If you're sincere, it's easy for you to get the support you need, because people understand how their actions fit into the big picture.

Matt talked to Tonya, a top-level manager, about projecting sincerity.

Matt: Why do you think sincerity is important in your job?

Tonya: As an executive, my staff members are always watching me for signals. If they think I'm not being honest, they get confused and upset.

Matt: How can you make sure you're projecting sincerity?

Tonya: The best way to project sincerity is to be as honest as possible. It's also important to communicate as much as you can. I also try to express my feelings so the employees get to know me better.

Matt: What about communicating issues that you know will upset your staff?

Tonya: I'm not doing people any favors if I hide information I think they won't like. It's better to just come clean with bad news. I just try to be sensitive and avoid embarrassing anyone with confidential information.

Tonya and Matt discussed the delicate balance that she has to ensure in order to communicate effectively. It's important to be open and honest, even in potentially negative situations. After all, she's not being honest if she doesn't occasionally show frustration or concern. However, Tonya must also make sure that she doesn't embarrass any of her staff members or put them on the spot while she's communicating.

If Tonya acts sincerely, there will be a match between her private and public self. When there is a discrepancy, it means she's hiding information or feelings, which can damage her leadership abilities.

Question

Susan manages a team consisting of several people. How can she integrate nonjudgmentalism, perception, and sincerity into her leadership style?

Options:

1. She should accept her team members on the basis of what she's heard about them in the past.

2. She should make her team members feel appreciated.

3. She should avoid articulating goals that her team members don't agree with.

4. She should try to understand her team members' feelings.

Answer:

Actually, she should accept her team members on the basis of what they can offer right now and she should make them feel appreciated. She should try to understand their feelings and communicate clearly.

Option 1: This answer is incorrect. Susan should not evaluate people on what may or may not have happened in the past because that may inhibit how she views their current performance.

Option 2: Correct. Being an emotionally intelligent leader means that Susan makes her team members feel appreciated. By treating them with courtesy and respecting their skills and personal lives they will know she values them.

Option 3: This answer is incorrect. Susan should not avoid articulating goals that her team members don't agree with, because they will have to deal with it eventually and putting off telling them will not make things easier.

Option 4: This answer is correct. Susan should try to understand her team members' feelings because being emotionally intelligent means she doesn't embarrass any of her staff members or put them on the spot while she's communicating.

Your attitude toward the people who work for you determines your behavior. If you look at your staff members with respect and a sincere desire to help them succeed, you'll make the first step toward leading with emotional intelligence.

Remember, it's important to provide support and avoid judging others as a leader. Your acceptance and honesty are the foundations to your success.

Problems come up at work constantly. People look to their management teams to resolve problems effectively. How can you ensure that you're taking the right approach?

Your ability to resolve problems effectively is key to your success in management. Employees will look to you to set a strong example. You'll explore:

- why it's important to take responsibility,
- how you can ensure that you're getting the right information,
- why communication is critical during problem resolution.

Sarah is the CEO of an Internet service provider. She is called on to solve a wide range of problems on a daily basis.

See each step for information on how Sarah tackles tough issues.

Get involved right away

"It's important to get involved right away. I don't procrastinate or hand the problem off. I make myself available as soon as possible."

Gather information

"I get first-hand information about what's going on. I don't rely on any one individual to inform me. I listen to all the perspectives."

The information you gather about a problem will ultimately determine the resolution you select. If you use effective information-gathering techniques, you can ensure that you'll make a better decision.

Read about each of Sarah's information-gathering techniques to learn more.

gathering information

"First, it's important to gather as much information as possible. I make an effort to talk to everyone who's involved, not just the people I already know. I ask everyone questions. I avoid assuming that there's a bad guy or that people I trust will have all the information I need."

delaying judgment

"I don't make a judgment until I have all the facts. It's easy to jump to conclusions based on a little information, but these kinds of snap judgments are often incorrect. Besides, if I make conclusions early, I may overlook new information that would change my decision."

making exceptions

"Sometimes, I have to extend a deadline or make an exception until I know all the facts. If I run into a problem on a project, it's better to wait until I understand the issue fully, even if it means extending a time frame."

getting specific facts

"It's important to make sure that people are specific. They often say things like, "She dropped the ball," or, "He hasn't been pulling his weight." I need specifics, such as, "She didn't turn in the report," or, "His project was four days late." Otherwise, I'm just dealing with opinions."

It's important to approach the problem-solving process with an open mind. As you move closer to a decision and action, your attitude will make a difference.

See each tip to learn how Sarah approaches her decision-making.

Be sensitive

"Sometimes, big problems are disguised as smaller ones. I always think through the effect of a situation. I once found a billing error that seemed simple. It turned out that our accounting system was corrupt and needed to be updated."

Stay open

"It's important to stay open to suggestions. It's easy to take the attitude that there is only one right solution. My staff members are a lot closer to technical issues than I am. I need to listen carefully to their suggestions at all times."

Make it clear

"I have to help all departments in my company understand the challenges we're faced with. I also have to make sure they understand our goals. This way, they'll know when they see an obstacle because they know where we're going."

Why is communication so important during problem resolution? Because problems frustrate everyone. People often lose their perspective when they run into hurdles in the workplace. The more clearly you communicate your approach throughout problem resolution, the more you'll help others stop focusing on frustration. You'll help them begin looking toward solutions and the future.

Your communication style sets the standard for how those you lead share information. You have an opportunity to set the example for smooth communication for those you lead.

Question

Brandi manages a loan processing division. She found out that several customer applications had somehow slipped through the cracks last week. These applications were never processed. Brandi needs to find out more about the issue. How should Brandi take responsibility and communicate her findings?

Options:

1. She should talk with the people who were involved.

2. She should ask a third party to investigate the problem.

3. She should let her staff know what her approach will be.

4. She should rely on the information senior level processors give her.

Answers:

Actually, Brandi should get the input of everyone who was involved. She should communicate how she will approach the problem to her staff.

Option 1: This answer is correct. In order to take responsibility, Brandi should talk with the people involved because going directly to the source will ensure that she will get accurate information.

Option 2: This answer is incorrect. Brandi should not ask a third party to investigate the problem because she would not be close enough to the information to make a clear judgment.

Option 3: Correct. In order to communicate effectively, Brandi should let her staff know what her approach will be because the more clearly she communicates her approach, the more she'll help others stop focusing on frustration and look for solutions.

Option 4: Incorrect. Brandi should not rely on the information senior level processors give her because if they were not the ones processing the applications, they may not have any more information than she does about what went wrong.

Your approach to problem solving will make a significant difference in your leadership abilities. Strong managers take responsibility for the issues that arise in their workplaces.

Communication goes hand-in-hand with problem-solving skills. The more clearly you express yourself, the better you'll be able to implement solutions.

How do exceptional leaders inspire others? Why do people enjoy working for a charismatic manager?

The best leaders inspire people beyond meeting goals to a strong enthusiasm for their work. They help their employees create a vision for the work environment. You'll examine:

- how leaders build loyalty;
- why a no-nonsense approach is powerful;
- how self-confidence leads to high achievement.

Retaining employees is one of the biggest challenges facing managers today. The best leaders build loyalty among their employees, which goes a long way toward reducing turnover. Wynette is CEO of a software development firm. Her employees are extremely skilled and it's important that she keep turnover to a minimum.

See each of Wynette's strategies for building loyalty to learn more.

Make a contribution

"It's important to let people know that they're making an important contribution to the company's bottom line. I make an effort to thank people for what they've done. I tell them how they've made a difference. When I give people an assignment, I tell them how their work affects the company."

Give support

"The best way to build loyalty is to support my employees. This can include funding or internal political support. My staff members can't accomplish their goals unless I'm behind them providing the resources they need to get things done. If I don't support them, they'll get frustrated."

Express warmth

"I let my employees know that I appreciate them. There are a lot of ways to express gratitude. I can write personal notes, leave voice mails, or send e-mails. I also invite employees out to lunch or have team parties to reward large efforts."

An important part of being a leader is building confidence. Leaders must help their employees have confidence in management, the company, and themselves.

See each characteristic for one of Wynette's comments about self-assurance.

Calm

"I approach our toughest projects calmly and with confidence. I let my employees know that they have the skills to get the job done. If I'm hesitant or nervous about a project, my staff picks up on these feelings. I project confidence."

Encouraging

"I encourage my staff to reach for tough goals. I support people in striving to be above average. I let them know that it's OK to take risks, and that I won't punish them when they've made good-faith efforts. This helps them achieve and develop their skills."

Inspiring

"Sometimes, times are tough and we can't afford more equipment or staff. I encourage people to dig deeper into their resources to meet goals. I do the same myself. It's important to lead by example."

Involved

"I stay very involved in day-to-day operations and I let my staff members know how much I care about what's going on. If I don't care about our work, how can they? I explain our goals and let them know how we're doing."

Many top executives have a quality that's often referred to as zeal. They enjoy their work and take pride in their accomplishments. They're also able to work effectively with others.

See each characteristic for more information about zeal.

See job as fulfilling

These leaders see their work as fulfilling and satisfying. They take advantage of their time on the job and stay involved in the day-to-day aspects of the business.

See others' perspectives

These leaders handle conflict well because they can see things from other people's perspective. They encourage other people to have open minds.

Kim and Todd discussed her no-nonsense leadership approach.

Todd: You've said you take a no-nonsense leadership approach. What do you mean by that?

Kim: Primarily, it means that I care about concrete results. I care about making a difference to the bottom line.

Todd: How do you communicate this attitude to your staff?

Kim: I support my employees as much as possible so they can accomplish their goals. I don't say one thing, then do another.

Todd: What do you expect of your staff members?

Kim: I expect them to use their resources as efficiently as possible. Sometimes, times are tough and they'll have to work more hours to get the job done.

Todd: How do you inspire your staff when times are tough?

Kim: I lead by example. I don't ask them to do anything I won't do myself. If I ask them to work more, I do too.

Kim takes a no-nonsense approach to management. She doesn't ask her staff to do anything she doesn't do herself. She supports her employees so that they can get their jobs done. She doesn't distract them with unrelated goals or projects that don't contribute to the bottom line. Kim gives her employees the resources they need and expects them to meet their goals.

Managers like Kim help their employees focus on getting the job done. A no-nonsense approach means supporting employees and moving toward concrete goals.

Question

Practice what you've learned. Identify the aspects of loyalty, boldness, zeal, and self-assurance necessary to the emotionally intelligent leader.

Options:

1. You should provide employees with the resources they need to get the job done.

2. You should set concrete goals for your staff.

3. You should only communicate about issues that directly concern your employees.

4. You should set intangible goals so employees won't feel threatened.

Answer:

Actually, you should support employees by providing them with the resources and information they need to get the job done. You should work toward concrete goals.

Option 1: Correct. Being emotionally intelligent means you provide employees with the resources they need to get the job done. The best way to build loyalty is to support your employees because without it they will get frustrated.

Option 2: This answer is correct. Being an emotionally intelligent leader means that you set concrete goals for your staff because it is important that they know what is expected of them and what is important to you.

Option 3: This answer is incorrect. If you only communicate about issues that directly concern your employees, they will not have the same commitment as they would if they understood how their effort benefited the company overall.

Option 4: This answer is incorrect. Emotionally intelligent leaders should not set intangible goals because this will not motivate their employees to strive for success.

Your ability to inspire your employees is important to your leadership success. Remember, the strongest managers are able to build their employees' loyalty because of the support these executives provide. They strengthen people instead of tearing them down. A no-nonsense, but caring, approach is the best way to organize and motivate an effective team.

DEVELOPING YOUR STAFF

Developing Your Staff

Emotional intelligence is critical to managers who want to develop good relationships with their employees. But how can you apply emotional intelligence on the job?

You can apply emotional intelligence every day on the job. One of the most critical aspects of emotional intelligence is your ability to develop and help others. You'll examine:
- why delegation is important,
- how you can delegate effectively,
- how you can help employees work toward long-term goals.

A key role for leaders is developing their employees. Why is it important to develop your staff members' skills?

See each benefit for more information.

saving time

Developing your employees is one strategy for saving time. As their skills increase, they'll be able to do their jobs more quickly and efficiently. You'll be able to hand off tasks that meet the skill levels of your staff, which will free up your time.

improving your team

When you give your staff members new and challenging assignments, you'll increase their skills. People will improve as they gain experience with new skills and knowledge. Your team will be better equipped to handle problems and challenges.

focusing on critical activities

When you develop your team, you'll increase people's skills. They'll be better able to handle the challenges they face, which will free up your time. You'll have more time and energy to devote to more critical activities because you'll spend less time on other tasks.

You'll put your emotional intelligence to the test when you work to develop your employees. You will use your communication and problem-solving abilities constantly. Delegation provides a foundation for increasing employee skills. You'll also examine how you can work with staff members to achieve their long-term objectives.

"I know I need to increase my emotional intelligence," said Debbie, a human resources manager. "But I don't have time. I'm too busy!"

Debbie is extremely busy--but she doesn't have to be so overwhelmed. An important step to developing emotional intelligence as a leader is delegation. You'll explore:
- why delegation is important,
- what issues you should consider before you begin delegating work.

As people climb the corporate ladder, they often become overwhelmed by the number of goals they are faced with.

Review each benefit of delegation for more information.

making time for your priorities

When you delegate assignments, you can concentrate on the more important tasks of management. These may include long-term planning, dealing with crises, and communicating with customers and other members of management.

developing your staff

When you delegate assignments, you create opportunities for people to learn new skills. If you hoard all the challenging work, your employees will become bored and restless. If you delegate, you'll also have time to coach your employees toward improved performance.

developing yourself

You won't increase your skills if you're spending too much time on a lot of tasks. Through delegation, you can free up time to attend training and receive coaching on your skills. You'll also have time to touch base with staff members in order to identify areas needing improvement.

Debbie asked for Rick's advice about delegation. He explained that she needed to think through several issues before she began delegating assignments to her staff.

See each factor for one of Rick's comments about delegation.

Objectives

"What are the objectives for the task you're assigning? What is the purpose of the work? You need to clearly define the objective for staff members before they start work. Otherwise, you won't get what you want."

Priorities

"Make sure team members understand their priorities. They need to be clear about how the new assignment fits in with their other tasks and where their primary concentration should be."

Communication

"Build up communication with your team. Encourage people to come to you when they have questions or run into obstacles. Keep apprised of what's going on, but avoid "checking up" on staff."

Trust

"Select people you trust. Don't just pick whoever is available to do the work. You should use the time you've freed for other things, so it's important that you're able to rely on your team to complete the task."

Doug talked with Karen, his boss, about delegation.

Karen: It's important that you start delegating some tasks. Have you thought about what you could hand off?

Doug: I think I can probably hand off the quality reports. The team leaders could do those, which would free up several hours a week.

Karen: What are your objectives for the reports? What should the team leaders focus on?

Doug: My objective is to understand our error rates. The reports help us track error rates. When rates increase, we need to do some problem solving.

Karen: Good. What about the team leader priorities? Where do the reports fall? Doug: They need to consider the reports a high priority. Mentoring new employees is the highest priority, but the reports are a close second.

Karen: Do you feel like you can trust the team leaders to take care of these reports? Do you have confidence in them?

Doug: I've thought about that. They'll take care of the reports. I don't think I have anything to worry about.

Doug thought through his objectives for the assignment. He also chose people he knew he could rely on to complete the tasks. It's important that he clearly communicate his objectives. He also needs to explain how the quality reports fit into the team leaders' priorities. Finally, he needs to establish communication channels so the team leaders get the support they need.

Question

Practice what you've learned. What are the important issues to consider in delegation?

Options:

1. your objectives for the assignment
2. identifying team members who have time to work on the assignment
3. techniques you can use to check up on employees
4. ways you can establish communication with your staff

Answers:

Actually, it's important that you think through your objectives for the assignment and how you can establish communication with your staff. You should also consider team members' priorities and who you trust to complete the assignment.

Option 1: This is a correct answer. One important issue to consider when delegating is your objectives for the assignment because unless you clearly define the objectives for staff members before they start work, you won't get what you want.

Option 2: This answer is incorrect. When delegating, don't simply give the work to someone who is free. The individual might not be the right person for the job and you may end up completing the task.

Option 3: Incorrect. You should not consider the techniques you can use to check up on employees because this seems like you do not trust them. In order to effectively delegate, you need to trust the person to whom you are assigning the work.

Option 4: Correct. You should consider the ways you can establish communication with your staff. Encourage them to come to you when they have questions or run into obstacles. Keep apprised of what's going on, but avoid "checking up" on them.

Delegation is an important tool for developing both you and your employees. You'll provide them with challenging assignments and you'll ensure that you have time to concentrate on other tasks.

Before delegating, you need to think through your objectives and priorities. It's important that you give clear, manageable assignments.

"I need to assign Cynthia to a project, but I don't want her to feel overwhelmed," said Frank, an information systems manager. "How can I make this go smoothly?"

Delegating effectively is a challenge managers face daily. If he follows some guidelines for effective delegation, Frank can ensure that the assignment goes smoothly. You'll examine:

- why it's important to get input from staff,
- why it's important to provide upfront information,
- how you can provide support while the work is going on.

Clear communication is the foundation for effective delegation. You must establish channels to communicate with your staff throughout the assignment. You need to make sure staff members understand projects and receive the support they need while they are completing tasks. Afterward, you'll want to discuss the success of the project.

You must clearly define the "target" for employees. What do you want them to do? When does it need to be done? What's the budget? Who can help? What should the final product look like? Give people time to ask as many questions as necessary. It's better to spend time upfront clearly defining your expectations than to run into frustration down the road.

Remember, the clearer you are upfront about your expectations, the more likely it is that you'll get what you want. After all, employees probably won't hit a target they can't see.

Delegation can be rewarding for everyone if it's done correctly. Managers free up their time and employees develop new skills. However, it's important that executives delegate effectively.

Andrea manages a group of engineers. She delegates regularly to her staff Select each factor for one of Andrea's recommendations on delegation.

Importance

"Employees need to know where their work fits into the big picture. I explain how each task contributes to our company and department objectives. Without this information, their work seems unimportant."

Timeliness

"I clearly communicate when I expect employees to start and finish work. I've found that timelines are often a source of misunderstanding. I get out a calendar and discuss exact dates for starting and finishing so there's no confusion."

Authority
"I let employees know the limits of their authority. In other words, I tell them the circumstances in which I expect to be notified. I don't want to be involved in the minor decisions, but there are times when I need to be consulted."

Resources
"I like to give employees a sense of the resources they can turn to. Not just budgets and personnel, but a list of people who have done similar work. I also recommend books or training that may help them accomplish their goals."

It's important for your staff members to receive feedback about the success of their efforts. Explore each phase to learn how Andrea evaluates her employees' success.

Throughout the project
"I set periodic milestones when I assign a project. I meet with employees to discuss their success so far. We can correct problems early this way."

At the end of the project
"I do a formal review of each employee at the end of the project. I let the employee give feedback about what I could've done better."

Question
Practice what you've learned. Darren is learning more about the importance of delegating. He's identified several tasks that he can assign to his team members. How can he delegate these tasks effectively?

Options:

1. He should establish how and when he will communicate with the staff.

2. He should evaluate the staff's success based on a review of what they've accomplished.

3. He should encourage staff members to set their timelines.

4. He should clearly identify the limits of his staff's authority.

Answers:

Actually, Darren should clearly establish communication channels and identify the limits of employee authority. He should evaluate success based on predetermined criteria. He should determine the timelines for staff members.

Option 1: Correct. Darren can effectively delegate by establishing how and when he will communicate with his staff. This is the foundation for effective delegation. Make sure staff members understand projects and that they receive the needed support.

Option 2: This answer is incorrect. Darren should not determine his team members' success on what they've accomplished, but on a predetermined set of criteria.

Option 3: This answer is incorrect. Darren should not allow his staff members to set their timelines because he will be able to guarantee the task will be completed on time. Rather to be effective he should set the timelines for his staff.

Option 4: This answer is correct. In order to delegate tasks effectively, Darren should clearly identify the limits of his staff's authority. He should communicate to his staff the circumstances in which he expects to be notified.

Your emotional intelligence is important to your success in management. When delegating tasks, it's critical that you use all your problem-solving and communication skills to make the assignment a success.

When you begin delegating, you'll develop both yourself and your employees. You'll have more time to spend on critical projects, and your employees will build new skills.

"I manage a large group of customer service representatives for a financial services firm," said Brad. "A lot of them want to become certified financial planners. How can I help them work toward that goal? Our company doesn't have a formal training program."

As an emotionally intelligent manager, it's important that Brad work to develop his staff members. Brad can help his employees by working with them to set goals and achievement plans. You'll examine:

- how to develop a goal plan,
- when rehearsal is effective,
- how to provide reinforcement.

A goal plan will help you and the employee work toward achieving results. This plan will break large goals into manageable steps. It will also detail the commitment both you and the employee are making.

Goal plans are appropriate only for large goals that will be accomplished over long periods of time. These plans aren't a good match for smaller tasks.

Margaret developed a goal plan with Fred, one of her employees. She followed a process for developing the goal plan.

Explore each step and example of how Margaret applied the step to Fred's goal plan, in order, to learn more about the process.

1. Detail the goal

In this step, detail the goal. Use only one major goal, such as "moving into a supervisory role," or "switching to the customer service division." These should be goals, not tasks.

Example - detail the goal

"Fred wants to move into an assistant supervisory position. He's currently a processing representative. An assistant supervisor title would be the next step in his career."

2. Actions required

What are the steps involved in reaching the goal? Some may sound overwhelming to the employee, but he'll see that you're making an effort toward his development.

Example - actions required

"The steps for Fred's goal are to attend supervisory training, achieve a 95 percent error-free rating, work on at least two department projects, and be recommended for the promotion."

3. Employee's commitment

What actions does the employee need to commit to in order to reach this goal? Which steps are the sole responsibility of the employee?

Example - employee's commitment

"Fred needs to take responsibility for achieving the 95 percent error-free rate. He'll also have to commit the extra hours it takes to work on department projects and attend training."

4. Manager's commitment

What can you, the manager, do to support the employee? Which steps in the development plan are your responsibility? What commitments do you need to make?

Example - manager's commitment

"I need to commit to giving Fred some free time for working on department projects. I'll also have to approve his training and be responsible for recommending him for a promotion when the time is right."

Rehearsal is another way to help employees meet goals. This technique is appropriate when a staff member wants to try a new skill and needs practice. Rehearsal is effective only for one skill, not large-scale goals. During a rehearsal, the employee tries the skill. You provide feedback--either by responding as if it were a real-life situation, or by telling the employee what might happen next.

Beth has to talk to a co-worker about clearing her work station. She is afraid the conversation will be difficult and has asked Jared to rehearse the discussion with her.

Jared rehearsed a discussion with Beth.

Beth: I could tell her that the general work areas need to be kept clean and that her help is needed.

Jared: What if she then says that she's so busy that she can't worry about keeping her work station clean?

Beth: I could tell her that keeping the work stations clean is an important priority now that customers are coming into the office more frequently.

Jared: That's a good way to approach it. The more you bring customers into the picture, the less she'll feel like it's a personal attack.

Beth: That's true. I shouldn't say that people have been complaining about the mess she makes. If I bring up customers, she'll see the value of what I'm saying.

Jared helped Beth think about how she would approach the woman in her office. Since Beth talked with him, she realized that her approach would make a significant difference to the conversation. This rehearsal doesn't guarantee that Beth will be successful, but it does increase her chances.

A final technique you can use to help employees reach goals is reinforcing appropriate behavior. You can use this technique when someone is trying to change a habit. For example, Ruth, a retail saleswoman, is trying to learn to control her temper during difficult customer interactions. Her boss, Andrew, gave her positive reinforcement when she handled a difficult conversation calmly.

See each of Andrew's tips to learn more about this technique.

Reinforce consistently

"I watched for instances in which Ruth was confronted by an upset customer. I made sure that each time she stayed calm, I praised her. I didn't want to ignore her efforts to improve herself after she had one or two successful attempts."

Reinforce in a timely manner

"I made sure that I praised Ruth as soon as possible. That way, the incident was fresh in her mind. We could also discuss how she handled the situation and the specific effective actions she took. The praise doesn't mean nearly as much a few weeks after the event."

Make reinforcement meaningful

"It means a lot to Ruth when management notices her improvements. I also began letting her train on another product line after she became competent at handling conflict. That way she can see that her behavior change led to positive events."

Question

Practice what you've learned. Julie is a manager in a retail store. She wants to help her employees develop. What techniques can she use to help employees plan and achieve goals?

Options:

1. She can use goal plans to help employees prepare for a specific task.

2. She can rehearse a specific skill with an employee who's preparing to use it.

3. She can develop a goal plan with an employee who wants to achieve a large goal.

4. She can provide positive reinforcement for employees who are trying to change a behavior.

Answers:

She can use goal planning to help an employee achieve a large objective. She can also use rehearsal and positive reinforcement techniques.

Option 1: This answer is incorrect. Julie should not use goal plans when preparing for specific tasks because they are far too detailed for single tasks.

Option 2: Correct. Julie can use rehearsal to help employees plan for a specific task. This is effective because the employee tries the skill and Julie provides feedback-- either by responding, or by telling the employee what might happen next.

Option 3: This answer is correct. Julie can develop a goal plan with an employee who wants to achieve a large goal. This is effective because she and her employee can break down the goal into manageable steps.

Option 4: This answer is correct. When developing her employees, Julie can provide positive reinforcement for a change in behavior. If she reinforces consistently, in a timely manner, and uses meaningful feedback, it will be effective.

A critical part of emotional intelligence is the ability to develop others. There are many tools you can use to help your employees move forward in their careers. You can develop goal plans to help people move toward an achievement. You can rehearse specific skill sets. Finally, you can help an employee implement a new skill by providing positive reinforcement.

INCREASING OTHERS' EMOTIONAL INTELLIGENCE

Increasing Others' Emotional Intelligence

As a leader, you're responsible for developing and motivating your team. You know that in order to perform effectively, each individual must have the ability to increase his or her emotional intelligence. How can you help make sure your team is emotionally intelligent?

One of the key components to increasing emotional intelligence is conflict management. If you can help your teams work through problems effectively, you'll be able to help them increase their emotional brainpower. You'll explore:

- how you can bring perspective to emotional situations,
- what you can do to calm emotional people,
- how you can be a supportive listener.

Question

What is the value of increasing other people's emotional intelligence?

Options:

1. You'll increase your staff's ability to cope with conflict.
2. You'll decrease the need for coaching.
3. You'll motivate your team.
4. You'll increase your team's technical skills.
5. You'll decrease the time lost in unproductive conflict.
6. You'll guarantee that staff members enjoy their jobs.

Answers:

Actually, you'll motivate your team and you'll improve your staff's ability to deal with conflict. You'll also reduce the time lost in unproductive contact. You'll still need to coach team members.

Option 1: This answer is correct. One value of increasing other people's emotional intelligence is an increase in their ability to cope with conflict. Working through problems effectively will help your staff increase their emotional brainpower.

Option 2: This answer is incorrect. As people's emotional intelligence increases, their need for coaching stays the same because coaching will always be important.

Option 3: This answer is correct. Increasing your team's emotional intelligence will motivate them because they will be equipped to bring perspective to problems and help people sort through their issues.

Option 4: This answer is incorrect. Increasing your team's emotional intelligence will not increase their technical skills because it is meant to help them increase their emotional brainpower.

Option 5: This answer is correct. By increasing your team's emotional intelligence, you will decrease the time lost in unproductive conflict because they will learn to work through problems effectively.

Option 6: Incorrect. Guaranteeing that your staff members will enjoy their jobs is not a value of increasing others emotional intelligence. Rather increasing your team's emotional intelligence can help them work through problems effectively.

You'll act as the voice of reason for your team. You'll help calm emotions before they erupt. You'll bring perspective to problems and help people sort through their issues.

Have you ever spent time with a sad person? Or an angry person? Did you ever feel like his bad mood was contagious?

Moods can be like colds--they "catch." When one person is feeling a strong emotion, the mood can spread to other group members. As a leader, you want to make sure that bad emotions don't extend throughout your team. You'll examine:

- why it's important to differentiate between your emotions and those of others,
- what you can do to prepare for emotional conversations,
- how you can alleviate anxiety.

An important first step in increasing the emotional intelligence of others is to manage your own emotions. As a leader, you'll often have to deal with tense or anxious staff members. You need to understand their emotions and help them cope, without becoming upset in the process.

The best way to manage your emotions during a difficult conversation is to prepare in advance. You may know ahead of time if you'll be facing a tough interaction.

If you prepare yourself, you can approach the situation rationally instead of emotionally.

See each technique for preparing yourself to learn more.

Anticipate feelings

If you know you have to meet with someone who's emotional, try to figure out how she's feeling. Is she angry? Frustrated? Sad? Consider her personality and how she has reacted in similar situations.

Decide on an approach

Based on the emotion you think the person will feel, decide on your approach. Should you be rational? Sympathetic? Does the person respond to facts or does she react better during an empathetic discussion?

Look for clues

Sometimes you won't know the person well enough to anticipate her reaction. In that case, you'll need to observe her behavior and formulate quick reactions. Listen to her tone of voice and watch body language for cues about emotions.

Question

One of your co-workers, Dawn, is extremely angry about the mandatory overtime your department is now required to work. Late hours will be required of everyone during an upcoming holiday weekend. You have lunch with Dawn and another woman who vent about the inconvenience. After spending time hearing about how angry they are, how do you think you'll feel?

Options:

1. not angry at all
2. a little angry
3. angry

4. fairly angry

5. extremely angry

Answers:

Strong emotions are easy to "catch." Often, if you spend time with a person who is feeling strongly, her feelings will begin to rub off on you.

It's easy to let other people's emotions get to you. To avoid this reaction, it's important that you differentiate and separate feelings.

Explore each kind of emotion for more information on how to differentiate them.

Other's emotion

Recognize how the other person feels: "Greg is depressed. He's feeling hopeless."

Your emotion

Separate the other person's emotions from your feelings: "Although Greg feels down, I am happy. I feel hopeful and upbeat."

Theo and Gwen discussed staying calm during difficult conversations.

Gwen: You had to talk with Dennis when he was upset. How did you keep things under control?

Theo: Well, first off, I knew he would be angry about a problem he was having. So I was prepared for his behavior.

Gwen: Didn't you dread having the meeting if you knew he was upset?

Theo: I tried to think about how to handle his anger ahead of time. I already had my reaction prepared. I stayed calm and said the things I'd rehearsed. I told myself that I knew Dennis was angry and that I wouldn't let myself get angry in response.

Question

Practice what you've learned. Identify the characteristics needed to manage an emotional situation.

Options:

1. You should try to understand the other person's emotions.

2. You should avoid "catching" the other person's emotions.

3. You should "mirror" the other person's emotions.

4. You should develop a strategy to handle the other person's emotions.

Answers:

Actually, it's important to avoid "catching" or "mirroring" others' emotions. You should differentiate between their and your feelings, and develop a strategy to handle the emotional person.

Option 1: This answer is correct. In an emotional situation, you should try to understand the other person's emotions because this will help you determine the best approach to take when dealing with that person.

Option 2: Correct. In order to manage an emotional situation, you should avoid "catching" the other person's emotions by reacting calmly and smoothly, and separating their emotions from your own.

Option 3: This answer is incorrect. Mirroring another person's emotions will only serve to complicate the situation. You should avoid mirroring the other person's emotions.

Option 4: This answer is correct. When attempting to manage an emotional situation, you should develop a strategy to handle the other person's emotions. Based on the emotion you think the person will feel, you should decide on your approach.

In leadership positions, you're often faced with talking to emotional people. To manage these interactions effectively, it's important that you can manage your own reactions.

To react calmly and smoothly, your best approach is to recognize the other person's feelings and separate them from your own emotions.

Has one of your employees ever become extremely emotional? Were you struggling to find a way to calm him down so you could solve the problem?

People become emotional at work--sometimes for good reasons, other times for reasons that are hard to understand. You may find yourself in the position of being the voice of reason. You'll examine:

- techniques you can use to calm an emotional person,
- how you can redirect the person away from the upsetting event.

The first step in dealing with an upset person is to cool him down. He may be yelling, cursing, crying, or shaking. When someone is in this mode, it's difficult for him to even communicate the problem. Your role is to get him to a place where he can talk about what has made him so emotional.

Question

How would you complete the following sentence?
When someone is upset, telling her to calm down:
Options:
1. will help her relax and focus on the problem.
2. will probably just make her more upset.

Answers:

Actually, telling someone to calm down will just upset her more. It may make her feel like you're not taking the problem seriously.

Option 1: This answer is incorrect. When someone is upset, telling her to calm down will not help her relax and focus on the problem. To help someone to relax, you should sympathize with them.

Option 2: This is the correct choice. Telling her to calm down when she is upset will probably just make her more upset because she will not think that you are interested in her problem.

When you're talking with an upset person, sometimes you have to help her get calm before you can have a rational conversation. Sid often has to help employees calm down.

See each calming technique Sid often uses to learn more.

Sit Down

"I ask the person to sit down. Sitting is a resting state and the person's heart rate will lower. If he stands, it's easy for him to get more agitated and pace. If he sits, he'll begin the physical process of calming down."

Timeout

"I offer the person time to catch her breath. I don't always make the offer directly. I might say, "Can you hang on a second while I put this in the mail?" Sometimes, this little break goes a long way toward calming her down."

Slow Down

"Sometimes, the person is speaking so fast I can't understand what he's talking about. I often say something like, "I can see that you're upset and I really want to understand the problem. Can you start over and speak a little more slowly?""

Calm Down

"Sometimes, I just offer the person a drink, like coffee, soda, or even some ice water. This effort lets her know I'm concerned. It also helps her begin to calm down physically, which is the first step toward mental calmness."

Sometimes, even if the person is calm, you'll have to help the conversation move forward. See each technique Pam uses to redirect the conversation for more information.

Interrupt

"There are times when I have to interrupt the person. He may be repeating himself or I can see that as he talks, he's getting more upset. In these cases, I say, "I'd like to interrupt for a second." This stops his train of thought and I can move the conversation in another direction."

Offer a different viewpoint

"There are times when I try to give someone a different perspective on the problem. This is helpful when the person's looking at an issue in black and white terms. I may say, "Have you thought about it this way?" or, "Here's another way of looking at things.""

Find help

"If the person is very upset and I can see that she needs help, I ask, "What can I do to support you?" Sometimes she needs mentoring, additional resources, or time. In other cases, she may just need someone to listen to her."

Diane talked to Chuck, who was very upset.

Chuck: I can't believe these technology support guys. I've left five messages and they still haven't done anything about my computer!

Diane: You sound really frustrated. Why don't you take a seat and tell me what's going on?

Chuck: My hard drive crashed and crashed. I keep leaving messages or waiting on hold. It's been hours and I haven't gotten any help.

Diane: I know how irritated you must be. But I can't understand you. Could you slow down a little and explain what happened?

Chuck: Well, I had two hard drive crashes. I've lost some material. I really need them to fix the problem, but I haven't gotten any response.

Diane: Would you like me to get involved? I could make a follow-up call. Chuck: I think that would really help. Maybe you can get them to pay attention.

Diane began by using calming techniques with Chuck. She got him to slow down enough so that she could understand him. She also offered sympathy and asked Chuck how she could support him. Chuck was relieved that Diane was getting involved with the problem, because he wasn't having success on his own.

Question

Grace is talking with Stuart, who just lost a half-day's worth of work because of a computer crash. Stuart is extremely upset and is yelling. Grace needs to calm him down before he disturbs the entire department. What can Grace do to calm Stuart?

Options:

1. She should ask him to be calm.

2. She should give him a "timeout" so he can take a few deep breaths.

3. She should ask him to speak more slowly.

4. She could redirect the conversation.

Answers:

Actually, Grace could calm Stuart down by asking him to speak slowly, inviting him to sit down, or giving him a "timeout." She could also redirect the conversation.

Option 1: This answer is incorrect. If Grace asks Stuart to calm down it will most likely make him even more upset because he will think she doesn't care or understand.

Option 2: Correct. One of the calming techniques Grace can use is to give Stuart a "timeout" so he can take a few deep breaths because this break will go a long way toward calming him down.

Option 3: This answer is correct. A calming technique Grace can use is to ask Stuart to speak more slowly because if he is talking quickly she may not be able to understand what the problem is.

Option 4: Correct. One calming technique Grace could use to calm Stuart is to redirect the conversation. If he continues to get more upset as he talks, she should stop his train of thought and move the conversation in another direction.

Work can be an emotional place. People often get overwhelmed by their feelings about co-workers, projects, or problems. You have an opportunity to help them increase their emotional intelligence in these situations. Your first goal is to calm people when their feelings are out of control. You can then move forward by getting them focused on solutions.

Have you ever been upset and turned to a mentor? Have you ever wanted someone with the power to help you to listen to your problems?

As a leader, you have an opportunity to help others solve their problems. You can provide support and direction by paying attention and offering helpful guidance. You'll examine:

- why your listening skills are important,
- how to follow a process for listening,
- how to ask thought-provoking questions.

You may have heard that good listening skills are a critical part of effective leadership. How do your listening skills help you be a better manager?

Read more about each function for information about the importance of listening.

Support

When you listen, you can provide support for employees during difficult times. The simple act of listening can be a big help to a stressed-out person.

Development

Listening can also be a development tool. When you listen and respond, you'll be able to help employees learn from their experiences.

By using a process for listening, you'll ensure that you're making the most of your interactions with employees. See each step in the supportive listening process for more information.

Paraphrase

When you paraphrase what you think the person really means, you help the other person clarify his thoughts. You restate in your own words what you think the person is saying. You might say, "It sounds like you're saying that you feel overwhelmed with the new project." You then give the person a chance to verify what he's said.

Share perceptions

Let the other person know what you think she's feeling. You'll get feedback about your perceptions. You may think someone is angry, when she's really feeling hurt. You'll also let her know how she appears to others.

Ask purposeful questions

Ask questions that help you better understand the situation. You may ask questions like, "What are your thoughts about...?" or, "What do you see as the pros and cons...?" or, "What information do you need to make a decision?" These questions will also clarify the other person's thoughts.

You can help the other person clarify his thought process by asking questions and giving feedback. However, it's important that you don't judge or evaluate the other person.

Review each tip for more information on supportive listening.

Don't Judge

Don't imply that you're judging what the person is saying. You can share your perceptions, but don't indicate that you think the person is right or wrong. Make it clear that your perceptions are yours alone.

Don't Be Negative

Avoid giving the impression that you think someone is right or wrong. Pay attention to your tone of voice and body language to make sure you aren't sending a negative message.

Don't Challenge

Avoid challenging statements that might make the other person defensive. Comments such as, "You're not making sense," or, "You don't get it," will only make the conversation deteriorate.

Don't Misunderstand

Make sure that you're perceiving the other person's feelings correctly. Check frequently by asking questions like, "I sense that you're angry. Is that true?" This way, you'll ensure that you understand the other person.

Question

James is talking with Connie about a conflict with a co-worker that has upset her. He wants to be helpful. How can James apply supportive listening techniques to the conversation?

Options:

1. He should ask Connie purposeful questions.
2. He should evaluate what Connie is saying.
3. He should paraphrase what he thinks Connie means.
4. He should share his perceptions of the problem.

Answers:

Actually, James should paraphrase what he thinks Connie is saying. He should share his perceptions and ask questions. He should avoid judging or evaluating Connie.

Option 1: This answer is correct. To apply supportive listening techniques, James should ask Connie purposeful questions. This will help him better understand the situation and help Connie clarify her thoughts.

Option 2: This answer is incorrect. Applying supportive listening techniques does not include evaluating what Connie is saying. Doing so will give Connie the impression that James thinks she is right or wrong.

Option 3: Correct. James can apply supportive listening techniques by paraphrasing what he thinks Connie means. He should restate in his own words what he thinks Connie is saying and then give her a chance to verify what he has said.

Option 4: Correct. James can apply supportive listening techniques by sharing his perceptions of the problem with Connie because he'll get feedback about these perceptions. He'll also let her know how she appears to others.

Supportive listening is a tool you can use to mentor your employees. When you listen and guide, you provide support and help other people develop. When you listen, avoid being judgmental or negative.

Effective listening skills are critical for leaders at every level. You'll find that supportive listening is an important tool for interacting with your employees.

Emotional intelligence is increasingly recognized as an important skill for leaders at every level. In this course, you've examined a step-by-step guide for increasing your effectiveness as a leader. You explored proven techniques for improving your relationship with your staff. You also explored leadership strategies for getting more work done with less stress.

REFERENCES

References

- **Constructive Thinking** - 1998, Epstein, Seymour, Praeger Publishers
- **Emotional Intelligence** - 1995, Goleman, Daniel, Bantam Books
- **Working with Emotional Intelligence** - 1998, Goleman, Daniel, Bantam Books
- **Measuring Emotional Intelligence** - 1997, Simmons, Steve M. and John C. Simmons Jr., The Summit Publishing Group,
- **Emotional Intelligence at Work** - 1998, Weisinger, Hendrie, Jossey-Bass, Inc.
- **Putting Emotional Intelligence to Work** - 1998, Ryback, David, Butterworth-Heinemann

GLOSSARY

Glossary

A

Adrenaline - Epinephrine. Something that excites or stimulates; an energizer.

Amygdala - A brain structure of the limbic system that is involved in emotions like fear and aggression.

Anxiety - Distress or uneasiness of mind caused by fear, leading to obsessive thoughts.

E

Embedded - Contained or implanted as an essential or characteristic part.

Emotional brain - The amygdala, which is that part of the brain involved in emotions like fear and aggression.

Emotional intelligence - Intellect that is determined by emotions like self-control, persistence, impulse control, and empathy.

Empathy - The identification with, or vicarious experiencing of, the feelings and thoughts of others.

Engulfed - Feeling overwhelmed.

H

Hippocampus - A curved ridge in the lateral ventricles of the brain, which is part of the limbic system.

I

Impulsive - Actuated or swayed by a particular feeling or mental state.

IQ - Intelligence quotient. An intelligence test score that is used to measure intellect.

N

Negotiating solutions - The ability to prevent conflicts or resolve those that flare up.

Neocortex - The bulb of tissues, making up the top layers of the brain, that regulates rational thinking.

Neurobiological - The branch of biology that deals with the anatomy and physiology of the nervous system.

O

Obsession - The domination of one's thoughts or feelings by a persistent idea or image.

Organizing groups - The ability that involves initiating and coordinating the efforts of a network of people.

P

Perseverate - To experience the uncontrollable repetition of a thought or idea.

Personal connection - The ability to use empathy and connecting to recognize and respond appropriately to people's feelings and concerns.

Physiological - Dealing with the functions and activities of organisms.

R

Rational brain - The neocortex, or bulb of tissues that make up the top layers of the brain that regulates rational thinking.

S

Self-aware - Being aware of both your mood and your thoughts about that mood.

Social analysis - The skill that enables an individual to detect and have insights about people's feelings, motives, and concerns.

T

Tunnel vision - The inability to see beyond a preconceived notion.

W

Worry - To feel uneasy or apprehensive.

Printed in Great Britain
by Amazon